Find Your Spark

7 Steps to Ditch Stress and Ignite 🔥 Your Financial Lifestyle

by RaShida Roberts

ISBN: 978-1-7367477-0-4

Publishing Support Services By: Motivational M.D. Publishing
www.motivationalmdpublishing.com.

Printed in the United States of America

I dedicate this book to

the Angels in my life who taught me how to laugh, cry, and still walk with my head held high. Who helped and rallied for me through my transformation of finding my voice. To the people who walked with me through the barren moments. Who challenged my thinking, and kept me moving forward. Who loves me and supports my financial journey. You have followed me and listened to many of my anecdotes about money!

Some of you have endured my passenger seat coaching! God bless you! May He continue to provide, protect, and give you peace in all financial matters.

I send you all my love: Mom, Jasper, Sunjanel, Alana, Shannon, LaTika, LaWanda, Uncle William, and (rip) Angel.

In memory of Grandma, Virginia Roberts, who first put the 110mm film camera in my hand sparking my interest. Who paid for our items in cash with your navy blue coin purse as we walked the country town streets. Who led a simple life, worked hard, was God fearing with a dash or two of hot sauce in her spirit.

Rest in peace. I love you always.

rest in peace to my Angel

Contents

Acknowledgements

Birthed from failures, cloudy paths, stress, financial flaws, determination, inspiration, courage, pain, positive thinking, grit, and the audacity to show up in my own life and now yours, I wrote this book! To God be the glory through all trials and triumphs. I'm grateful that I was able to get to a place to write this book. The pandemic of 2020 carved out a key venue for me to do just that.

First, I want to thank my mother for writing her book—a devotional, *Every Day with the Gospel of John: 365 Days of Devotions and Prayers,* and for being an inspiration through her writing journey. She has embodied traits that I continue to strive toward every day. Her dedication to her tasks and follow-through are extraordinary. She is laser-frig-gin'-focused, y'all (LOL!). Anything she sets her focus on, she completes. I thank her for her encouragement and for listening to my financial advice (I have a lot of advice. LOL!). I look forward to reading the legacy she has written for the life of Christian believers. I know she has devoutly tried to live a life worthy of His calling, and that is a sight to see up close and personal. Mom, I'm thankful for the prayers you have put in over the years and spiritual discipline, a devout Christian and a woman of God's own heart! You have been someone that I can always look up to, even through difficult times! Thanks, mother dearest, for all your wisdom, selflessness, and strong will! I love you!

I especially want to thank my brother, JMoe, for supporting every opportunity I presented. He is always the first person to help his family and friends.. While writing his music and producing two music albums for his label, Made Guys Entertainment at www.madeguysentertainment.com

he supported me throughout my journey. Having someone in your corner when you have your doubts is a blessing indeed, especially when it's family. If you like Hip-Hop/Rap, check him out at **bit.ly/jmoemusic**! Thank you for your love and support, bro! There are not many made like you. You are indeed a great provider, supporter, and talented young man. May God continue to direct you and bless you. I love you!

Another huge shout-out is to my Day One, Janel, who encour-aged me through the entirety of my book! It was pure seren-dipity that we reunited before the pandemic. God works in mysterious ways. If it were not for her amazing friendship, I could not have made it through this book and the year 2020! So many storms hit me. Her angel wings lifted me when life took my breath. When I should've given up on life, she was there in support, never sugar-coating. I can't tell you how many Facetime dates we had during which we stayed up to work together, each on mute. I remember those nights when I was still going strong, and she was tired but got out the bed to see me through. She listened to my dreams, excuses, failures, frustrations and still pushed me toward my goals! I learn from her every day. She's a God-send lifelong friend and a great example of what it takes to be successful. She's my secret coach! I couldn't have finished this book without her helping me, rooting for me, and believing in me. She blessed me beyond measure in getting my book published, and I'm forever grateful. Love you to pieces.

During the early stages of my financial journey (long before COVID-19), I visited my dear friend, Shannon, who has always been an oasis of wisdom and faithful friend. On that visit, I struggled to choose to stay an extra day or two or leave due to finances. I was embarrassed for myself. However, I'm thankful she let me be transparent without feeling like a total failure or less of a person or friend. From that day, I never wanted money to be the defining factor in spending time with loved ones. I didn't make changes at that time, but the fact that I vividly remember how it felt to penny-pinch while on vacation is enough to commit to never wanting to be in that position again. Our memories and the time we spend with others are more important than what we accumulate to make us feel something. Shannon is the person who, for the past several years that I've known her, had checked on me at the oddest of times when life looked bleak. Unknowingly, she saved me from my discouraging thoughts at times. She has the gift of honesty, encouragement, and patience—lots of patience (How I do not know!)! Thanks for checking on me and keeping our endless conversations going! Kisses and hugs to your five precious heartbeats. Thanks for y'all's hospitality each time I see you. Love you, friend!

I'm grateful to Alana for always keeping her door open. I never (and I mean never) have to sugar-coat who I am or what I've done with my Ace! She keeps it all the way real! We grew up on that motto! Thank God for who she has been to me over the years and for seeing me through a rough patch while writing this book! It's not every day your friends swoop in and clean and check things out when you can barely hold yourself together. We've come a long way, and I can't wait to see how we continue to grow. Love you dearly.

Another friend who helped me get over a significant hill is Archie. I appreciate you, sir, for being honest. Having honest and open conversations has been the crux of it all. I appreciate you and love you!

You think when you're at a certain age (and an educator at that) that certain issues wouldn't be an issue. Unfortunately, life happens to us all, and it's up to us to meet the challenge or fold. When you have friends that help you along the way, it's more than a blessing.

Since I was a child, there has always been one God-sent family member who was kind, listened, and supported me. That's my Uncle William! I don't know how much he knows this or how refreshing it is to have a soul such as his life. We don't talk much, but I can still remember the day he helped me solve a geometry proof in the ninth grade. The way he explained it opened up my world in math that year! I was so grateful, relieved, and excited. I *loved* geometry. So much so that I took Pre-Calculus in the twelfth grade. That was a long time ago, but he is constantly dropping nuggets of knowledge with his laid-back persona. My favorite saying from him is, "What happens at the top, happens at the bottom." I often repeat this phrase, which means don't be impressed by people buying impressive things. People who have a lot of money struggle the same way as people at the *bottom* of the socioeconomic ladder; it looks slightly different and has a higher price tag. Such advice gives me the power to write without regret. To be open without grief. To go forth and just do what I need to do. Thank you, Unc. Love and appreciate you!

Another helpful family member is my firecracker cousin LaWanda (and my other cousin, Latika)! Hunnie! Wanda listened to *all* my tea. When you have financial struggles, it's not about the finances. Rarely are money issues about money; they are about everything else going on in our lives. And I tell you, the years leading up to this book were not always kind. I'm thankful that she was a listening ear with solid advice, not the kind that just goes along with what you say, but one who challenges your thinking and helps you look at things differently. I love her brutal honesty and quest to have peace in her life. We all should have people in our lives that make life fun, can turn up, but also keep it real at the same time. Thanks for your support, cuz! I love you. Latika, I love you too!

To tackle this book, I wouldn't have been able to stay up endless nights and days if it weren't for my study fur baby, Angel. She passed away abruptly, and that halted my writing. I did not do anything for at least a solid month. I've never come home to such an empty house in my life. The energy was not the same, and it never will be. Sometimes I find myself saying, "This day would be better if Angel were here." I honestly believe my financial stability could've prevented her sudden death, which is part of why having your finances in order matters. Proverbs 12:10 says, "The righteous care for the needs of their animals...," and I tried to do that to the best of my ability. You never want to look back and think that money was the cause of why you couldn't save someone or something you loved. That's heartbreaking. It's hard to forgive yourself, but you must. I did.

Nonetheless, she kept me company, believe it or not, until the end. That drive to the emergency room was our last drive cruising down the streets. The crisp night was perfect weather, unlike most August evenings. It was quiet and serene, a calm drive. She was having difficulty breathing but still managed to take her last peek out the window and rest her head on the car while the wind embraced her face one last time. Then she peeled back to rest her body in my lap as we drove to the emergency room. She gasped for her last breaths the entire time. I thought everything would be okay. We always made it out of the emergency room just fine. Instead of coming back to me, her lifeless body was rolled out on a shiny silver tray, covered in medical blankets. We sat outside, on the side of the building alone in the early hours of the morning. I rocked her back and forth in my arms, wrapped her in one of our favorite blankets, then left. That drive home was the loneliest, and when I crossed the threshold of my house, the emptiness was overwhelmingly crushing. I was crippled. I cried ugly tears. I screamed, and then I cried some more.

Angel was a symbol of love and kindness. She brought smiles during the dark and gloomy periods of my life. We were two peas in a pod, and I took her everywhere I could manage. I never knew her death would have such an impact on me. We never know how God's creatures will show up in our lives. I mentioned my loss to a student one day after school when we bumped into each other at the dollar store, and she said, "Well, maybe it's time to make room for more." I don't know what that "more" is, but I'm genuinely thankful for the experience of having, caring for, and being a steward over one of God's creations. I will *always* love and miss my Angel. Rest in peace.

Before writing this book, I hadn't thought about all the financial lessons I've learned over the years. I'm very blessed for people like Granny (my dear friend Brittney's grandmother), who taught me some basics about stocks in our Ladybugs Stock Club when I was in the last year of my teens. Granny and the Adams family have always supported me, and we have been family friends for a long time. They have helped me when I was fundraising for my school, classroom, or another non-profit. And they helped me with my new business, Ginscookies! I can't count how many times I showed up unannounced and embraced with open arms. They've seen me through a lot of good and bad times. Thank you. I love each one of you: Britt, Cheryl, Brittney, Alexis, Kaylee, Ava, Pippen Dana, Uhma, and Uhmpa, Bubba, Robin, and the rest of the family!

In addition to the Reids, Henry A. and Valencia, thank you for introducing me to a financial literacy program that prompted my thirst to learn more about financial matters. Val, thank you for your support and friendship over the years. I wish nothing but God's blessings for you!

The beginning of this book began at Taurea Avant's Book Camp Boot Camp. I wrote the outline and a lot of content for my book. Taurea showed us how to promote our books, print our books, and continue to leverage our books as entrepreneurs. I am immensely grateful for the information that I received. That camp put me on the path to successfully writing a book! Thank you!

Thank God for all my trials and errors with money, from moving back home in my twenties to paying off debt, taking money out of retirement accounts, to all my old and new friends (who left an imprint on my heart, and family members who jumped on board in supporting my new lease on life. Everyone couldn't make it to this new season, but I continue that the Almighty will bless and protect them.

Jassy Dallas Childs (www.FabulistaCookies.com) and Yvonne Brown (www.affirmandpursue.com), thanks for always being Queens of encouragement and lifting me in the name of the Most High. Yvonne and I successfully launched and crushed our first venture together (www.reigniteyourfinances.com), and I can't wait to see how God uses us in the financial literacy space. I am coming for everything God has set in my heart and mind! Brandy Black, we are going to make it! I declare it! I'm blessed to still know my opera camp friend from middle school. Peace and blessings to you, dear friend and thank you for the support. Tiesheen, love you to pieces! Thank you for your encouragement. Alicia, thanks for being a jewel from day one and being force of enlightenment! And I want to thank

Alondra for her tenacious spirit surrounding investing. You are indeed a financial inspiration, and so many people will build wealth from your expert tips (www.mamabearmentors.org). Finally, I want to thank the Black Women Empowering Finances organization (www.blackwomenempoweringfinances.com) for coming together and creating a safe space for small business owners. Financial Experts Tashaya Singleton and Dee Bowden have truly blessed me over the months I've known them. I learned a lot of great information from you both, along with Joyce Chesley Hayward and Janisha Richardson. Each of you ladies has been a blessing to me on this journey.

There are many people with whom I connect through social media, networking, programs, and day-to-day conversations, which have helped me to write this book. George Dines, Shawn Milton, Darryl Woods, Stephanie Carter, Tiffany Largie, Markeda Maxie, Sanah Bittaye Mitchell, Teasha Jenea, etc. Most of those conversations continuously confirmed that I should publish my book. I'm immensely grateful for those people who believed in this publication before it ever hit the shelves! Thank you for trusting my vision and for your support!

I'm humbled by the support I've received from many people. I want to thank Dr. Jasmine Zapata and the Motivational M.D. Publishing team for helping me to self-publish this book. Coach Julia was a blessing to consult with for my first book. I love the energy and uplifting atmosphere of Dr. Jaz's brand. Her words are inspirational, and from the first moment I met her, I knew she had a good heart and was genuine. She stands behind each author and rallies for us all to work together! Thank you!

I also want to thank the two people who make me look good, Rolanda Campbell, my hair and makeup stylist, with

Exclusive Beauty by Ro (www.exclusivebeautybyro.com) and Burl Hampton, III with 2902 Media (www.2902media.com) for his photography and videography expertise. Both worked with me, pushed me, and helped me out when the universe was trying its best to keep me down. I enjoy working with each of these jewels and their brand. I'm so honored to work with so many businesses that have great hearts.

Please find the list of additional supporters who believed in my project at the end of this book. Many of them have been a part of my story as they have encouraged me, listened to me, and we've discussed our struggles and triumphs, and encouraged each other in Christ. God bless each of them. To all my readers and supporters, may God's light shine on you, as well. Moreover, thank you to those who take the time to read diligently and take action. It's for you! Peace and Blessings to you all.

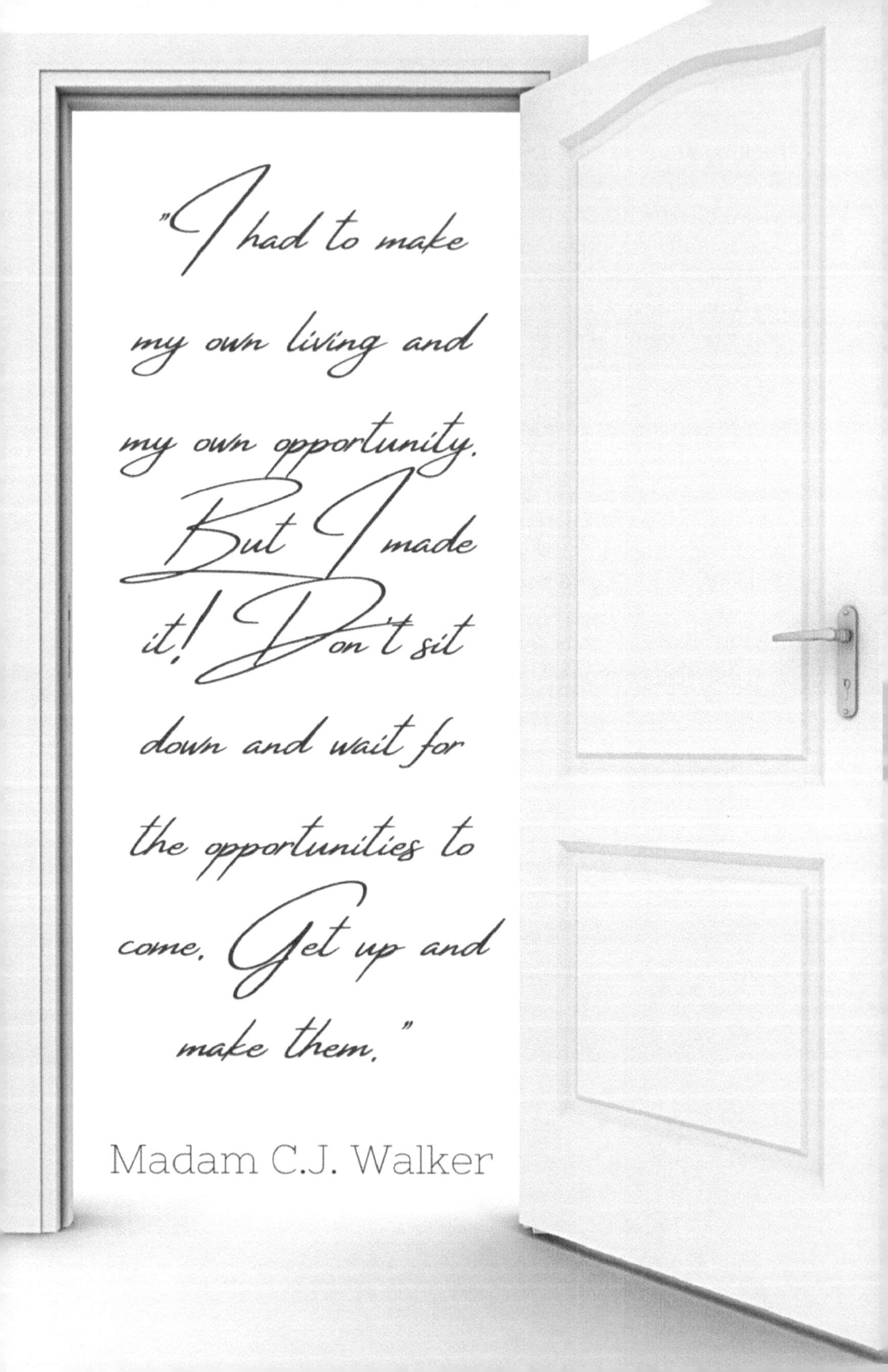
"I had to make my own living and my own opportunity. But I made it! Don't sit down and wait for the opportunities to come. Get up and make them."
Madam C.J. Walker

Preface

Congratulations on purchasing *Find Your Spark: 7 Steps to Ditch Stress and Ignite Your Financial Lifestyle*! Welcome to a movement of changing your mind so you can change your habits to ditch stress, ditch debt, and elevate your life!

I have taken bits and pieces of my journey to sculpt the framework of this book. It's dipped in childhood and adulthood naivete with key empowering moments of epiphany wrapped in a spark of hope! Some of you may remember the term latchkey. Well, that's how I grew up, as a latchkey kid, with a lot of alone time, learning how to figure out myself and the world around me. If you grew up in a single-parent home or in a home where your parents worked a lot to put food on the table, you could probably relate. So I've had to figure out money, have a strong mindset, and deal with emotions through my experiences and watching others.

I observed my hardworking mother, my friends, listened to the pastors in my life, read the Bible, and wrapped up those lessons into some kind of uplifting and wacky philosophy—which had major holes! Through pain, teachings, and inappropriate relationships, I learned to be a people pleaser. Those experiences made me ill-equipped for a world where I needed to use my voice, set boundaries (for my body and money), and deal with conflict maturely.

After going through back-to-back stressful situations resulting from bad decisions and experiencing failures, my finances were in red (I was overspending). I didn't know how much until I began to assess the situation in the summer of 2019. The bank always said I was overspending by so much each month when I logged in, but I didn't pay attention because the bill got paid on time!

For a moment, I felt defeated. For a moment, I was ready to break down and cry. For a moment, I wanted to cast blame, but the only direction I could point my fingers at was me. I made those decisions; I didn't use my voice, and I tried to please people. I used the money to run away from my pain. And so, I took full accountability for my actions and inactions.

What happened that was so tragic?

Well, I drained one of my retirement accounts and blew nearly $30,000 in three to four short years. I had nothing, absolutely nothing, to show for my $30,000 mistake. I had some great experiences but no assets and a lot of debt. There were mounds of unfinished hopes and dreams (grad school). Had I dealt with the conflicts in my life, learned to use my voice, and dealt with the low-key abuse from toxic people—all of which made me humiliatingly mute, I would be further ahead.

Once you start accessing the real causes of how and why you spend money, you will find its roots in behavior, emotional, and mindful experiences (good and bad). Money is emotional. Money is mental. Money is invasive. Until I dealt with my mindset, let go of the stress, let go of some habits, and let go of some people, I couldn't have conquered my money issues: paying off more than $15,000 in debt in my first year, paying off my car early, eliminating credit card debt, paying down a timeshare (an unfortunate decision I made during my walking dead era), budgeting and following a strategy, setting up my emergency fund which saved me several times early on—allowing me to stay on my debt snowball plan, learning how to budget better, and forming more positive relationships with experts, family, and friends about money.

So, I wrote this book to help you on your journey to ditch the stress, so your money choices will better suit you! I want my financial coaching clients to have a good idea of how they, too, can ignite their financial lifestyle and have a place to turn to when we may not be meeting face to face! In addition, I wanted a place to send my financial coaching clients to know that we all have some bite to our story before we begin targeting our financial success. It's time to let the smell of disappointment, the stench of debt, and the shame fade away. We can't stay in those moments.

If we knew when the end would come, if we could see who's really in our corner, if we could just envision the future, we'd have the strength to keep going and let go, then fast forward, and let God! Until you rid yourself of the stress in your life, dealing with money issues will be cyclical and a nuisance. I want you to be stress-free, so you can make logical decisions about money, create new habits around money, create a new mindset, and make a plan to ignite your financial lifestyle. Have fun and funds! You deserve both!

Money is like the thread of a blanket. It can't keep you warm by itself but shaped and sewn in the right hands, it'll give you a level of comfort you can't get without it. So, grab a pen and notebook to jot down your thoughts. This book is action-oriented, so I encourage you to journal about each part of the book and jot down your answers to the questions. I ask tons of questions to help you think through your situation. Discuss the book with family at the kitchen table, huddle up with friends, and challenge your partners and peers. If you take the suggestions in this book, you will be uncomfortable. It will make you vulnerable and push you to new heights. It is in these moments we find growth.

Introverts, don't be afraid. I'm going to ask that you push through and challenge yourself. Coach Roberts is speaking! Extroverts, hang in there with me. You're not off the hook, either; you, too, need a lesson in standing still. Throughout the book, I'm preaching, but it's coming from a place that wants the best for you.

Read and reread this book as many times as needed. Grab a trusted friend, go the distance, and try something different. Just ask yourself, "Is what I'm doing right now working? How well is it working out?" If you can stand to change a few habits and think differently to get to a better version of yourself, then read, write, think, do, and repeat while you read this book!

Don't forget to download any resources at bonus.findyour-spark.info. I look forward to hearing your reactions and anecdotes about how this book helped you in some signifi - cant way. I want to see the glimmer in your eye, the smile on your face, and feel the hope that lies within you when you cross the threshold of a stress-free and debt-free lifestyle! Let's get our spark back and add some fuel to it as we go!

"I would like to be remembered as a person who wanted to be free...so other people would be also free."

Rosa Parks

Introduction

Find Your Spark: 7 Steps to Ditch Stress and Ignite Your Financial Lifestyle is about changing your relationship with money by altering your mindset first. It's also about changing the behaviors that got us into our situations. It's about taking accountability for our actions and being proactive to help our problems. It's about navigating and understanding how our capitalistic society contributes to our mismanagement of finances. But more importantly, it's about YOU, showing up for yourself in ways you never have. I want you to crush your goals!

This book is for people struggling financially, struggling with stress. If you are ready to clear your mind of stress and get out from beneath the dark cloud of debt, then the ideas expressed in this book will put you on the right path when you take action.

As an educator, single woman, and Believer in God, I have developed my book to include Biblical references for singles and families who may struggle with the stress surrounding their lives and finances. Singles have to learn how to take care of themselves. Some of us have great families to help us during financial crises, but some don't have that luxury. We have to figure out ways to make it work—make us work to be as stable as possible. When we don't get up and get to the business of getting to business, we don't get paid, and then our problem can essentially become someone else's problem.

I have written this book as plainly and transparently as possible to help you understand that we all make financial mistakes. Throughout this book, you will find quaint anecdotes, handwritten pages of my journey, and humor and sarcasm. I know someone out there will be counting the prepositions at the end of sentences (I left those just for you! LOL!). Despite the many laughs and serious tones, if you're not afraid of growth, then this is the book to help you reach the next level beyond a financially stressed life.

I believe that you have to heal from within to improve your behaviors. You can't move one step forward physically or mentally if you don't take care of the thoughts and stresses in your life. Can you move forward without doing so, yes, but at what cost?

Though we are solely responsible for our behaviors, we must understand that our society has sensationalized fast and furious spending. In America, we are pumped from kindergarten to twelfth grade to go to college, get a job, get a house, a car, have kids, and retire, with each level adding more debt. However, we never learn many of the components surrounding how to be a fiscally responsible citizen and avoid the debt traps. We must understand the environment we live in so that we can prosper. Our minds must be free of stress so that we can think and move logically to stay out of the cyclical rat race so many find themselves in today.

Once I got the stress out of my life, it was easier to see and face the significant issues I had dug myself into financially. It was like a cloud of doom had been lifted from me. I took immediate action by starting a side hustle or two, finishing school, making some financial moves, educating myself about financial topics, and surrounding myself with others moving in the same direction. I couldn't believe that I'd let myself get to such an irresponsible place. But then, after digging even deeper, there were historical habits I had not addressed.

I focus on critical areas such as mindset, goal setting, having tough conversations, and being transparent with someone in your network. In addition, we will cover being proactive about the traps in your life, taking control of your life, using your time wisely, and learning how to conquer financial issues. These areas intertwine with logic, rationality, and your brainpower to make decisions that ultimately better your mental and financial health.

To get the benefits of this text, you have to be open to taking the challenges and answering the questions presented before you (grab your notebook). I give you a lot to think about by probing you with questions, some rhetorical. These are vital components to how I moved into a winning season over the stress I was carrying and the accumulated debt during those stressful years. There will be bonus materials in written format, audio moments to listen to, and moments to reflect and share your journey.

It's time that you get back to your true self. It's time to dig deep and be willing to let go of ideas, places, objects, and people that impede you. To attain a kindling spark of hope, you need to move on, move up, and move out to new territory.

To do so, you have to embrace and understand your personal, cultural, subcultural, and familial philosophies about money. You have to be willing to challenge, change, or work around some of the subliminal and overt messages you receive about money that isn't serving you, causing added stress and debt.

Every day we receive different messages about how we should handle our money, and these philosophies often collide, leaving us wondering what we should do. As you read, keep what's for you, and consider some new ideas. Each of the ideas in each chapter helped me to walk into a new era of my life. Your life will change, too, if you're brave enough to go the distance.

You will get specific information on how to make changes in your mindset, habits, and finances. For example, I discuss my C.A.S.H.F.L.O.W. method to get out of debt and move on to build wealth, my method on budgeting, increasing your cash flow, and beating some of your biggest challenges: credit, inflation, big business, and taxes.

If you can stand to make some significant changes in your life, then turn the pages with pen and paper in hand. Take copious notes, take defining action, share your pivotal moments, and don't look back! Find Your Spark is a continual process, but this book aims to give you the components and inspiration to light your fire!

"Find Your Spark"

I hear the laughs and the music
Outside my window.
I see the hard work and sacrifices
Next to my pillow.
A computer.
A desk.
A book.
A plan.
All meant to get me out
Out of this hand—
Of paycheck to paycheck,
And Sky high interest,
The hand of cards that has me
Stuck.
Stuck with what I witness:

From grief and migraines
That our money causes.
From debts on debts
That glitter our closets.
The Stress
The Toxicity
The Eviction
The Suicide Tendency.

The Adoptions
The Bankruptcy
The Criminology
We drown in Identity—

Showing up as someone else
To flex and to flaunt,

Other's names brand our Skin
To our people we Taunt.

WE NEED HELP!

To keep us off our knees.
From begging our Dear Lord
Cries to the banks and governments
Begging to our kin
Giving up our precious coins
To the Predators within—

Our Communities
Our Homes
Our Jobs
Our Nation.

Stealing our money
From all different places.
From Black Wall Street
From Taxes.
From Check cashing fees
Rent-to Own Entrapments.

From Redlining
From Big Business
From Predatory Lending
From Rapid Refunds
And all that is Trending.

Our Futures
Our Peace
Our Movement
Our Generations.

Will all be in Their possession
If we refuse our Inauguration.
The inauguration of
Assets over Liabilities
Literacy over Ignorance
Compounding over Saving
Charity over Indifference.

THEY

are not coming to save you.
To Drown out your Pleas—

YOU

have to save yourself.
Mindset reveals your choices
Change your actions into wealth.

We are changing our personal economies.
We are coming for our health
We are inviting quality people
We are rebuilding self

We will conquer our past mistakes
We will rid our environment of negativity
We will empower our families
We will drip our movements in unity

We can change our narrative.
We can take down establishments.
We can live in abundance.
We can be inhabitants—

With riches for our children's children
With wealthy legacies of yore
With stress free mindsets
With debt-free living in store.

I still hear the laughs and music
outside my window.
I understand these moments
But don't let my hustle dwindle.
Transformation
Justice
Impact
Millionaire status.
I embrace in my heart.
I am on a journey to wealth
To ignite changes which impart.

To Spark a flame and encourage your start.

CHAPTER I:

Mindset Matters

Your mind controls everything you do. What we feed our minds results in how we behave. In this chapter, we take a close look at how to shape our minds to receive more positive input, reject negativity, and begin thinking with a growth mindset. Understanding why we do what we do, checking ourselves, and allowing peace and serenity into our daily and weekly activities, and relieving stress in our lives are essential steps to healing. Your mindset is either keeping you running in place, tearing you down, or helping you to soar to new heights. It's your million-dollar asset. Every dream, goal, and desire happens first in the mind. Ditching your stress starts here. You cannot have a stress-free life without first being mindful of your mindset: Mindset matters most.

"Not everything that is faced can be changed, but nothing can be changed until it is faced."
James Baldwin

Permission Granted

You met your toughest critic the day you were born. They were with you during the best times and when you were at your darkest moments. They laugh at you when you try to move forward in life and remind you of the shameful acts you've committed. When you finally get the courage to do more, be more, your critic comes out to put you back in your place and question, *Who do you think you are*? That critic is you–the person keeping your mindset lagging instead of launching.

I get it: You may have made some significant errors, embarrassing ones, unbelievable ones, regrettable ones. You may have pushed them to the back of your mind or mulled them over like it happened yesterday. Horrifying mistakes that make you feel as if you are incapable of being victorious, experiences you may never want anyone to know about, and missteps that make your belly quiver like financial failures, bad relationship choices, trusting the wrong people, not speaking up on serious matters, and allowing acts against you or people you love. We tuck these moments in storage and try to forget about them, but somehow they find their way to the forefront when we apply for new adventures in our lives. When will we stop? When do you stop replaying the theatrics in your mind? It is time to forgive and stop punishing and resenting yourself for past mistakes.

We give too much power to our past pains. Many of us carry heavy loads drenched in deep, dark secrets wrapped in agony and regret. The weight of your past will drown every spark of hope you try to light until you face it and forgive. I can't stress this enough. I'm telling you that walking around with dark clouds over your head, refusing to deal with your problems, and conjuring up past mistakes over and over will lead you past stress into a cycle of blaming others and self-afflicting territory. Forgiving yourself (and others) is the single most challenging step to do and, simultaneously, the most liberating process to all that you want to accomplish.

The Bible says, "The tongue has the power of life and death." And that is true. As you reach out to voice the unthinkable, you're crushing every bit of the person you want to be, the person you could be. So, you may have a laundry list of mistakes like me:

1. pulled from a retirement account,
2. as an educator spent too much money on classroom supplies,
3. got talked into buying items you didn't need,
4. gave an offering out of a guilty spirit,
5. charged up thousands of dollars on your credit card,
6. let people close to you get over on you (i.e. family, friends, coworkers) or use you,
7. spent your hard-earned dollars on a significant other who ran out on you
8. trusted the wrong person,

Anything registered yet?

9. said something you wish you could take back,
10. held down your homies when you should've looked out for yourself,
11. shopped to impress someone when you didn't have the money,
12. didn't speak up when they touched you in-appropriately,
13. got scammed out of your money,
14. ignored signs in a bad relationship,
15. or didn't speak up when it counted (at work, home, etc.).

I've made plenty of mistakes, sins, or wrongdoings, whatever you want to call them, and more will transpire. We could go on and on about the mistakes we have made in all areas of our lives. We have the power to hold recurring dead thoughts in our minds and in the same strength to talk about a life of abundance and positivity. It's life or death. Which one will will you choose? Which one will encourage you to run towards your dreams, towards living stress-free?

Let's stop ourselves right now and say:

My past mistakes do not define me. My past mistakes do not determine my future. I will not let future mistakes halt my progress. I'm determined to do better. I am doing better.

How to forgive yourself:

1. **Face your issues.** Acknowledge what happened to you by writing down the experience or telling someone you trust (a counselor or a true friend). Once you get it off your chest, you will feel lighter.
2. **Forgive yourself.** Yes, you messed up. Say it out loud: I messed up. And then ask for forgiveness and make it right if the matter involves other people. Ask for forgiveness from God. Lastly, ask for forgiveness from yourself. Be sure to forgive yourself–for real this time.
3. **Move on.** We can only move on when we have granted ourselves permission to forgive and accept our consequences. When you move on, you're affirming what happened while understanding that you are still deserving of the successful treasures in life. Moving on is not constantly looking back to sulk, and it's not allowing our past to be held over our he by others (including self) who commit to loving us.

Moving on permits you to put on the armor of life and go forward with the hope, dignity, and confidence it takes to rock out your goals. For your sake and for those you love, move on from your past decisions. The stamina it takes to hold on to childhood problems as an adult, past mistakes, and what you should have done or said will keep you stagnant. Free yourself; it is the only way to live life more abundantly.

Write: What mistakes do you need to forgive yourself for? Who do you need to forgive? What past mistakes do you need to get over and release?

What's Buggin'?

Doctors cannot treat what they do not know. They can give you medicine for the symptoms, but they cannot heal the brokenness if they do not recognize the source of the problem. And it's unwise to operate without being able to see the totality of the problem. Such acts could cause more significant issues. Similarly, you cannot fix your overwhelming stress levels until you identify what's bugging you. Diving in and putting patches on damaged areas will only mask your problems, cause new issues, and worsen the real problem.

Identifying what is financially stressing you may not be what you think it is. Most of us may think we're just overspending. That may be true for many, but sometimes you need to dig a little deeper to find the missing puzzle piece to understand the source of your stress.

For example, I remember trying to get my issues with money together to see what key proponents were keeping me in debt. I wasn't *just* overspending; it's who I was spending my money on.

As an educator, I can recall spending cash on countless projects in my classroom, materials for my students, and decor to make my students feel comfortable. However, I can't forget about supporting every student club's T-shirt campaign, the fundraisers for students' hobbies, and buying supplies students couldn't afford. Did I stop there? No, because then I was buying into the sunshine committee, the teacher shirts, birthday collections, and school events like contests, field day, potlucks, paying to wear jeans, or participating in the dress-up day and Spirit Night! I spent $5000 on classroom materials my first year! And those were just job expenses. When I looked at my personal life,

1. I was buying gifts for people above my budget (wait, what budget?),
2. giving money to people for various reasons,
3. purchasing items on my card for "pay me back later" deals,
4. paying everyone's ticket to events, and
5. spending money to appease others.

I recall paying for gifts and bills in a relationship with money I didn't have (all credit cards). I was doing the most (for all of my adult life, it felt). And it was draining me. Can you imagine how many hours I had to work to pay back what I owed? That's the cost of overspending. Instead of enjoying what we purchased, we're stuck working at a job, which sometimes is the last place we want to be, around people who don't look out for our best interest.

All in all, it all came down to putting more energy, time, and money into everyone else than I was putting into me. Who else has spent $5,000 for classroom supplies in a tax year? Who else has spent thousands of dollars on girlfriends or boyfriends? But how much of that did I spend on myself? I didn't even have an emergency fund. My scanty savings account was nothing more than a placeholder for a few hundred dollars waiting for an ill decision.

I was giving, giving, giving, but I was not giving anything to myself! Once I decided where my stress lay, I was able to fix it. And basically, it came down to trying to help everyone else, not speaking up, and trying to look good in everyone's eyes. I'm such a pleaser. And it has gotten the best of me throughout my life. It seems innocent, but it's not if you're willing to dig deep. Pleasing others can get you into a lot of trouble. I'm often in disgust when I think back to crucial moments where my agreeable mentality got the best of me.

All in all, if you don't put a name to your stressors, trust me, you will be on the hamster wheel of repeating your mistakes. But once you have the anecdote to eliminate what's buggin' you in your life, you will gain success in health—financially, mentally, physically, and spiritually.

Write: What serious issues do you need to resolve or gain clarity on? Be honest.

Check Yourself

Our government is divided into three branches of government: legislative, executive, and judicial, to keep the economy running effectively and efficiently. No one party has too much power (*supposedly*). Thus, if there is an abuse of power in one entity, the other branches are deemed to step in and disrupt the flow of misappropriating actions (#blankstares). Checks and balances. The takeaway is that the government is set up to protect itself.

In the same manner, you have to protect your number one asset, and that's you. Sometimes we have to protect ourselves from outside advances, but we need to protect ourselves from ourselves most of the time! It's you, Bro! It's you, Sis!

We set up the most obstacles for our lives by not understanding who we are and not evaluating nor checking our toxic behaviors. When we own up to our story, we release the grips others think they have on us, we free ourselves of guilt and shame, and we understand our innermost being and purpose in life.

What is the foundation of who you are? What are you rooted in (your core values)?

Moreover, we need to reduce self-inflicted destruction like:

- Psyching yourself out of opportunities.
- Saying negative things about yourself.
- Surrounding yourself with people who don't like you.
- Comparing yourself to others.

You get the picture. That's toxic. And if you want a chance at ditching stress, then you better find a way to check yourself and scratch those behaviors off your to-do list.

How are you getting in your way? Is it self-confidence, addictive behavior, or pride? Think about your physical, emotional, mental, spiritual, and financial habits. What's stopping you from living the best version of yourself right now?

Be honest and dig deep.

Write: Take time to respond to the questions above.

Having a clear picture of who you are and dealing with stress will help you stop adverse reactions and thoughts. It's like hunting. You need a clear picture of your target, so you can aim and take down your prey. No one (on Earth) should know more about you than you. Sometimes that means getting the help you need to have clarity.

It would help if you also targeted your reactions to stress. I bet you'd find some key trends if you dived into your checking account. Our purchases often leave clues to our unhealthy choices and emotionally distressing situations. Detectives usually follow money to solve crimes. I think you will find some answers too if you do the same. You may shop a lot, eat out, buy junk food, go on trips to escape from home, drink too much, smoke, entertain yourself and others, or find other purchases that point to your stressful situation. Different reactions to stress could be devastating, such as psychological breakdowns, self-harming mechanisms, sleeping, distancing oneself, over-eating, lashing out angrily, experiencing headaches, stomach ulcers, or other excessive or damaging behavior.

Write: How do you react to stress-related events? **Take a look at your bank accounts.** What does your bank account say about you?

Pinpointing how you react to stress will give you more clarity to win your pressure battles in the future. If you knew the plays for the opponent's team before they played it, wouldn't that put you at an advantage? Let's take one of the most stressful seasons there is, Christmas. If you know you tend to shop or spend money carelessly during the Christmas season (*because everyone has to have a gift, right?*) and the like, you are more equipped to eliminate unnecessary expenses in the future by being aware of your behavior. Not having enough money during this season could add to the stress and pressure you feel about buying each person a gift. I made a choice to shop for kids only because I was in the habit of trying to ~~buy~~ please everyone ~~a gift~~. I recall having at least thirty to forty people on my list to shop for one year. Look, I'm one person on one teacher's salary trying to show I care with a gift that was costing me more than money. So, I stole from myself to make it happen. I stole my time. I stole from my investments. I stole from my future.

What are you stealing from yourself by not setting up the proper habits to divert bad spending? Stressful spending?

You have to take the necessary steps to curb your behavior. Get in front of the stressful reactions by putting in safeguards. You could make it harder to get access to your money by having two signatures on your accounts. You could put your money in an account that takes several days to complete the transaction (I do this with my emergency fund). You could start saving early on or buy presents throughout the year for special occasions. You can talk with your family and friends to let them know you're making some changes (and that you'd like their support, but it isn't required). There are many options you could try until you're strong enough to stop the stressful spending.

Write: What roadblocks do you need to set up to curb some of your bad habits? How do you spend your money when you are stressed? Who do you allow in your life to give you a dose of reality without the love, respect, or relationship shattering? Who's stepping in to stop you from your harmful reactions to stress?

Take time to check yourself, so you can be one up when temptation comes knocking. We win by being prepared (as best we can) for life's unknown challenges. And that starts with a good foundation: "A wise man builds his house on rock (Matthew 7:24)." Look within, get rooted in who you are, taking care of every aspect of you: the good, the bad, and the ugly.

I'm not there, YET!

There's a term out there in the education world that we call a growth mindset. Many people say it, but most do not adhere to it: I'm talking bosses, administrators, and leaders, even teachers and instructional coaches/specialists. If it's hard for trained leaders to keep up with this mindset, it can feel impossible for others to reach this level. Many of us lack how to maintain a mindset of moving past our current situations, pains, self-doubts, and stressors in life and continue moving forward to our desired outcomes. We wallow, we gossip, we shout it loud on social media, or we nurse our pains through other avenues. Those actions operate on a fixed mindset as if you can never get out of your current situation. For instance, your financial future will mirror that of your parents, you will never get a better job, you will always be living paycheck to paycheck, you will never pay off your student loans, your credit score will always be bad, or you will never obtain wealth or own your own home.

Stop.

Becoming fixated on such notions will never get you to the financial state you want for yourself, nor will it ever get you beyond the mental state you need to be in! Who lost weight by saying they couldn't? Whoever won an Olympic medal by weighing themselves down with *I can't* mantras? Have you ever conquered anything after you constantly told yourself you weren't good enough, worthy, or talented? I bet not. Could you imagine the posture it would take for a boxer or Olympic track runner to recite negative iterations to themselves while they trained for a competition, or better yet if they showed up to the event in that mind frame? That sounds a bit silly when you think of it, right? But we do it to ourselves *all* the time.

One of my good friends and I decided we would repeat a mantra from the movie *Cool Runnings* where the guys are trying to pump up one of their Olympic teammates. One of the characters, Junior, looks in the mirror (with his teammate coaching him) and repeats some encouraging words to himself until he believes them. Only then was he able to gather the courage to conquer his fear and take action.

The team also struggled to stay motivated because there had never been a bobsledding team in Jamaica. They were ridiculed and laughed at for having their dream. It came to a point where they had to choose: walk away or believe in themselves. They had to change their mindset, despite their dire circumstances, that they had just as much chance to win as any other team. **Spoiler alert**: Though they didn't win, having a growth mindset allowed them the confidence and the posture to say, *yes*, we can do this! But each person had to make that decision for themselves and erase fear and self-doubt in order for them to compete as a team. Y'all, most of our problems lie within us. But what are you going to do about it?

If you accomplished anything in your life, at some point, you stopped wading in the water and began swimming toward your destination. And that's what a growth mindset is all about. It's the ability to shape your world based on effort, not your current skill set or abilities, but your hard work, dedication, and perseverance. It's knowing that you can gain those skills. It's about gumption. It's about grit! The intention is to remain optimistic about what you CAN do to reach your goal. If you ever meet someone who embodies such a mindset, you will feel like a new person when you sit down and discuss your circumstances! Your conversations are different, how you act around them, and how you feel after you leave them is opposite from someone with a fixed mindset. Some of the best people I know who do this well are teachers, coaches, and parents! They don't let you sit in pity for long without suggesting or challenging you to look for solutions. The workload is on you. Such conversations will be refreshing from the right person! Go down the list of people you encounter daily and from time to time. Who are the people who leave you pumped?

Write: How many of these positive powerhouses do you have in your corner? Who would you say fits in the growth mindset category in your life? And then think of those persons with a fixed mindset. How do you feel around the person who has a fixed mindset vs. the person with a growth mindset? And then assess who you prefer to be around more often.

As you assess your friends, coworkers, or family members, don't forget to evaluate your habits. Because if you draw closer to the fixed asset people, then it may be because that's how you view the world. And suppose you cannot pinpoint one person in your circle that's a positive powerhouse (including yourself. In that case, it's time to cultivate a different attitude and actively seek out other *growers* to be in your top three persons of influence—people who have the most impact on your life.

Coaches: Business coaches, life coaches, success coaches, trainers, etc., do this well. They focus on the actions it takes to make you successful. They know weaknesses will be strengthened. A coach will push you beyond your capabilities. And when you look back, you'll be amazed at your achievements. A coach will push you, but do *you* push you! To reap the benefits of a growth mindset, *you gotta do the work*—the mental work and then the physical work. You cannot stay in *Stressville* and slurp stress soup, and sip stress tea, and think that you're going to slip out of your stressful situation.

Your finances will continue to look you up and down if you do not put in the work to change the status quo. Change your mind about financial matters: Avoid being another statistic who lives paycheck to paycheck, refuses help from financial coaches and experts, never educates themselves about how money works (it's more than just working and getting a paycheck), always borrows from friends, family, or the bank, and doesn't understand how taxes work in our country. You have to grow your mind to think differently about your financial situation. It COSTS YOU MONEY to be ignorant and even more money to stay there. You may not be there (financially stable) yet, but start thinking and planning how you can.

You have to think better to do better. If you cannot get your mind right, you cannot get out of your stressful situation. If you cannot keep your mind straight, you cannot avoid getting trapped in the maze of worry and anxiousness. Remember, it's all in the mind. Train it to think better: Say, *I can*. Say, *I will*. Say *yes* to more opportunities, and say *no* to negative thoughts and actions.

As you change your words, you will change your mind to live more intentionally and relaxed about your current life. As you begin to think and grow to be more positive, you will find yourself gravitating toward others who do the same.

The more you think along these lines, the less tolerant you will be of fixed mindset people. Try to have some grace once you arrive, because they too aren't there, YET!

I challenge you to get started! Take anything you want to do but have not been able to accomplish, write it down, and say, **YET**.

Write:

"I'm not good at ______________________________, **YET**."

"I'm not a ___________________________________, **YET**."

Always add the **YET** in there when you have those moments of despair or when you're unconsciously downplaying how truly awesome you are! **YET** affirms that you are continuously working on the issue, and you have yet to arrive. You cannot, and will not let inertia take place!

And when you're truly ready, add an *I am* statement that foretells your dream goals. You have to see it before you can do it!

I am a powerhouse.

I am stress-free.
I am a knowledgeable educator.
I am living the life designed for me.
I am an author.
I am an inspiration.
I am a phenomenal father.
I am a fierce mother.
I am financially stable.
I am a loved single.
I am a legacy builder for my family.
I am debt-free.
I am successful.
I am enough.

Write:

I am ______________________________________

Get it Together!

While writing this book, we are at the height of the COVID-19 pandemic. Fear and panic have caused most Americans to be without necessities like toilet paper, hand sanitizer, paper towels, and other household items. Why? Because people let their emotions take over, putting others at risk.

When you rule your life by unmanaged emotions, you are guaranteed to make ill decisions, putting your livelihood and others in danger. Making essential choices during periods of anger, depression, extreme anxiety, or fear can cause you to make some illogical and irreversible resolutions. Did you know that you are chemically imbalanced during these periods?

In a constant state of stress or worry, you may not be yourself. You could have difficulties making decisions, thinking, prioritizing tasks, and managing day-to-day life. When we are stressed out, we are vulnerable to being angered, saddened, and fearful. These emotions can feel so overpowering that they constrict us from performing at our very best. At some point, we have to stop and take hold of our emotions. We have to stop letting the small stuff or the big stuff overwhelm us to the point of physical and mental ailments. We have to GET IT TOGETHER!

A few techniques you can do to manage your emotions are:

Stop, breathe, and think. Pause everything that's going on around you and calm yourself down. Your actions may be different if you're in private vs. public, and it also depends on who you're around. Remember, you're still alive, and though you may not change the situation at that time, you will figure it out (growth mindset). I tell myself, you're okay, and keep it moving.

There will be times you have to set those emotions aside to take on reality and the day-to-day tasks before you.

There are times I have been flaming angry, and I had to check out to calm myself down. I rarely get enraged, as it takes a lot out of me. I don't like that person at all—she doesn't think well during those times, which is how I manage during extreme times to remain uncannily peaceful. Or sometimes, I'm shocked, which requires me to be mute to process what's happening. Because I know I can only deal with reality effectively when I'm thinking logically and unemotionally, I sort of check out. That's my body's way of reacting. Not everyone reacts this way, but some of us need to train ourselves to check out of the moment and gain clarity to gather ourselves. I usually choose to write to express myself because I can think more clearly. And so can you.

I urge you to get it together. Don't be ruled by emotions or stressful situations. You're the adult. Take charge and regain your composure, or don't lose it in the first place. It is far better for you to leave most situations until you can think through your next steps. That's easier for us singles;

however, running out the door could be seen as avoidance if you're in a serious relationship. The focus in such matters is to do what's right and what's best for you—that will vary for us all.

Time to Write!

Writing is truly a window into the deepest parts of your inner being. It is healing. It is cathartic. It is a road map to solving your problems, developing your master plans, and mastering your critical thinking skills. The one place you can show up to be genuine, authentic, and totally you is what you put down on paper. The experiences you will manifest by simply writing down your thoughts are transforming. I dare you to add this task to your regimen and watch how it helps you.

I've used sticky notes, journals, electronic notes, and napkins to get the stuff out of my head and in a place where I could visibly see it. I'm no doctor, but as an educator, I've learned more about my students and how to help them when I ask them to write open-ended. I invite you to do the same.

Warning: Make sure if you're writing about things that are sensitive, that you don't want anyone to know at a given time, safeguard it, or heck, in some of our situations, we shouldn't write it down at all (lol, I kid, but I'm not kidding.) or at least burn it up! I kid you not; if you leave it out by accident, you will be in a forced conversation that you may not be ready for but need to discuss.

On a serious note, writing down your thoughts gives you more clarity than you will ever have because then you can go back and pinpoint how you felt or thought, why you feel or think that way, and then make plans to change wrong thinking. I have had to look at myself with a side-eye after I've gone back and read some of the most nonsensical lines in my journal. What was I thinking? At the same time, I've looked back and have seen some of my ingenious thoughts. You will find gold if you take the time to write out your feelings. It will calm you down. If you don't want to use pen and paper, try the voice recorder on your phone and talk it out in privacy when you're driving home. Just be sure to safeguard these innermost feelings if you're not ready to share them with others. It happened to me, and whew, it wasn't pretty.

Journal Entry, 2017

> My why: ...Some of us are tough. We know we will get through it eventually. ...I'm here to be that person that I never had ...[or at least I thought]...but there has to be a wedge, a stone or something to stand firm with people who need a little encouragement. I am that wedge. I am the stone. That's why! People need help! They need help to be the best "me" they can be.

I encourage you to write, even if it's not every day: you can journal once a day, once a week, or after major and minor events in your life, etc. It could be when you're having trouble getting a hold of yourself or an emotional setback. Write, not only for pain but for pleasure, too! You've had some good moments, some wins, and some amazing thoughts. Remind yourself of the small blessings in life so you can smile when you look back.

Run!

Finding moments of peace and stillness in this chaotic world is a must. A chance to get away from the crowd, the voices, and the noise of everyday life will do more for you than some other forms of healing at times. It is not always possible to escape, but when and if you can, get out of there! *Run*!

The temporary escape will allow you to focus on calming down, breathing, listening to your thoughts and feelings, and making sense of all that has occurred. Removing yourself from situations allows you to think and act rationally. It enables you to gain your composure and mentally prepare how to resolve the issue. Now, I will say, sometimes running is an escape to avoid dealing with your emotions. If this is the case, you need to rethink this strategy. Don't go off running like Forrest in the movie *Forrest Gump* because you'll still have to return home to deal with the same issues. You're only putting off your problems and sometimes adding to your stress load.

I know because I traveled from place to place in 2017 to get away and find peace. It was peaceful away, but I still had to come back to deal with the same problems I left. Running away is a natural reflex of protection. For those of us who may have a foggy brain when overwhelmed with emotion, it's best to remove ourselves from that environment. Exit quietly and quickly so you can regain your temperament.

The same goes for avoiding people and places that cause you to have overwhelming emotional outbreaks. Why tempt yourself? Pass up that restaurant or outing where you know they will be, or change your route on the way to get the kids. Avoid places where you will be tempted to spend your last dime or swipe your credit card. Whatever you have to do that's within a reasonable amount of effort, please do it.

If you don't practice self-care with your emotions, who will execute this task for you? No one. It is your natural right and duty to promote a healthy emotional state and environment for your life. You are solely responsible for protecting your emotional well-being. So, run!

"Ummm"

We live busy lives. We're trying to take care of ourselves, be a good worker, a friend, a daughter, a son, a businessman or businesswoman, satisfy our significant others, be a good father or mother, pay the bills on time, listen to our friends, go to every event we are invited to, be informed about political happenings in our community, and so on. And that's just some of the positive tasks we are labored with each day. I'm tired just reading that list!

Imagine when things get over our heads, and we're not performing well. When our finances aren't enough, and we have mouths to feed, childcare to pay, rent and mortgages due, furbabies to care for, emergencies that eat away at our accounts, cars breaking down, or are diagnosed with an illness. It is easy to get overwhelmed by the day-to-day challenges that cumulatively disrupt our flow. You have to give it to yourself though, how many times did you conquer everything you needed to do when you were completely stressed out!

We can operate during turbulent times for a while, but not forever. The body, the mind, and the spirit need a reset to fight against a breakdown. You need to set aside the phone;

you need to block out some people and tasks in your life; you're going to have to say *no* to some events to gain some *ummm* time.

Yes, that's right. You need to set your *ummm* appointment. Whether you meditate, pray, read, clean, workout, listen to music, write, paint, bake, sew, throw around the basketball, run, hike, watch the sunrise, etc., you need a significant amount of time to find peace. The goal is to think clearly and openly without planning for some event or figuring out how to do this or that, taking everything that we need and want to do off our minds.

This is a must.

You need downtime to escape life's struggles and achievements. All stress is not bad, but we still must take time for ourselves. Even the busiest stay-at-home wife with four kids or the single dad or mom with one kid, the single entrepreneur with no kids, the educator, or the caretaker who's on duty 24/7, must find time to reset and balance. Think of the things you can do which make you happy and help you to get away from problematic issues that are going on in your life. Is it going to a movie to escape? Is it sitting in your car after work (in the garage before going inside (I love this!? Do you enjoy lifting weights? Running? Or how about walking down a trail or path? Is it baking? Do the sounds of rain or the ocean help you escape? Or is it sitting at home relaxing in a chair or listening to the silence and watching out your window? It can be simple; it doesn't have to cost money. I prefer that it did not cost you money or very little in the grand scheme of things, especially if your stress is financially motivated,

All in all, you have to find time for clarity. Often in these times, you're going to find what you're looking for. You're going to be able to create order from chaos. Your vision will come during these moments. Your clarity will come when you are focused on the white space. How many times have you been in the shower or relaxing unbothered, and that brilliant idea popped into your head?

Whenever you take your mind off the mountain, you will find your solution. Those are times when our most extraordinary plans come about.

Let's try saying it: *Ummm*.

Let's make plans to put down the phone, turn off the noise that keeps us rattled, log off of social media, drop the controller, and find a healthy and positive escape. And then, we're going to book that appointment on our calendars. Make this time intentional (Saturdays for me), and you'll find that you will handle the stress coming your way more effectively.

Write: In what ways do you need to show up for yourself when it comes to mindset and removing stress? When can you carve out some time just for yourself?

CHAPTER II:

No Target, No Success!

You can pick up a bow and arrow and shoot without looking, without aim. It's going to hit something, but what? Sometimes in life, no plan can land us in a fantastic opportunity or keep us spinning our wheels on the treadmill, going nowhere fast. It's like driving in neutral. How many of us are driving in neutral?

When it comes to money and living a less stressful life, we need to aim with a little more precision. Targeting your success is about making do with what you have, writing out your goals, planning for life's challenging moments, and celebrating wins! I believe even people who have success without plans have a plan of some kind. They target something, even if it is the smallest of ideas leading to something bigger and bountiful. Success comes when it's not only targeted, but the beholder remains steadfast and focused.

"I don't focus on what I'm up against. I focus on my goals and I try to ignore the rest..."
Venus Williams

Determine What You Can Change

The Word of God commands us not to worry. But often, we find ourselves pacing back and forth in our minds on how we can fix problems we can't ever change. We focus on the wrong targets and sometimes end up doing nothing. We have to point ourselves in the right direction. Being precise about what we *can do* will give us more success while pursuing our goals.

However, if you aim and shoot without a target, you will always miss the shot. How can you be financially free yet have no goals or strategies to get there? How can you lose weight without a plan to attack your situation? How will you become a better co-parent, friend, a project manager, scale the ranks at your job, fix your tardiness, find work, help your child, speak up, find new sources to fund your classroom, be more patient, or remove stress without first thinking, wanting to, believing in yourself, and taking specific steps to achieve your endeavors?

Doctors don't give you three magic beans when you are sick, and neither would you accept those beans when you're in dire need of an antidote. You'd probably be quite upset if they said, "Well, we hope it gets better," and sent you on your way. It's quite frustrating to be at the end of the tunnel with no recipe to follow. Where's the light in that?

Instead, doctors give you a plan and prescriptions to follow to heal your body. With that, you have tiny goals and tasks to complete, giving you satisfaction, relieving a certain amount of stress. In the same manner, you need to have a prescription, a plan, for your goals. Pinpoint the steps you will take to free yourself from your stressful situation and then execute.

Journal Entry, 2015

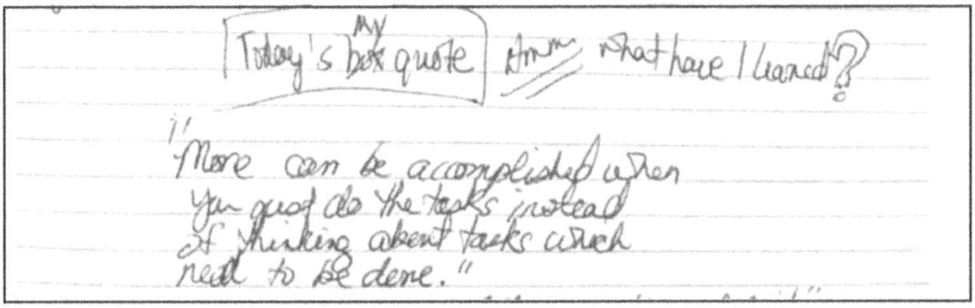

Personal example of what I need to do.

We're not blowing on dandelions or putting buttercups under our chins to get there, either. When you're targeting the actions you'll take to hang up your relationship with your stressors, you need to determine what you CAN fix and what you CAN'T fix. Don't set yourself up for failure. Why give yourself targets you can't hit? Especially when you haven't trained for the tasks? You would be wasting your time and energy and furthering your stress and anxiety. We have to focus on what we can change and build momentum to get there as well. And if we're honest with ourselves, we will find that we need to focus on our actions and behaviors, not the inaction of others. You cannot change other people. You can only change what you do (behavior) and how you respond (attitude) to life.

Most educators, coaches, and success-driven people will tell you to create measurable and manageable goals for yourself.

Your goals should be precise, suitable for your situation, traceable, and have a dedicated timeline to complete your goals. To be stress-free, you're going to have to sit down and determine what you can and are willing to fix concerning you. For more information about how to create your goals, you can go to bonus.findyourspark.info.

Write: What issues are currently stressing you out? Decide which issues are within your power to fix. What steps *can* you take? What steps *will* you take

Take Care of the "What-Ifs"

Some people say life is too stressful to be preparing for the unknown. That this kind of thinking means you don't trust God. I ask: Are we here by accident or by precision, carefully and methodically placed for a divine purpose? We can't plan every detail of our lives, but many areas call for planning. And if done, it would yield less stress. How many lives were saved years after Hurricane Katrina because of the plans established? What would a better plan for a worldwide virus outbreak have looked like for our country? Can you see it now? No plan is 100% accurate and secure, but without one, it can be devastating.

When you are stressed and overwhelmed, hanging by a thread, and relying on a cup of coffee to keep you going, preparing for the future is probably not on your to-do list. You're exceedingly busy dealing with present-day crises and trying to put out spot fires in your life to no avail.

If you want to get out of this mode and have more success over stress, you have to take care of the "*what ifs*" in life. There's nothing like having goals and being on your path to happiness when something unexpected arises, pushing you back down into a pit. It's devastating and causes you to move backward.

Two areas that cause dents in our plans are usually health and wealth. But if you secure some funds to cover health problems and emergencies, you'd be in a better position. Did you sign up for your Health Savings account or Flexible Spending Account? Do you have an emergency fund? Do you have auto and life insurance? Again, it's not going to be full-proof, but given the world we live in, would it serve you to have these in place?

Wealth does not extinguish the existence of diseases in our bodies. Still, it gives us a more robust platform to remedy such issues as they arise, or better yet, prevent them from appearing altogether. Ultimately, you want to be an emergency planner. Setting aside funds for quick and long-term emergencies will soften the blow that life will bring. Notice I said *will.* You *will* experience these complex trials (or lessons) in life.

Though we cannot prepare for everything in life (infidelity, addictions, family problems, rare illnesses, job-related issues, etc.), we could lessen our stress load if we could find the help and adequate resources, usually through being financially fiscal.

Journal Entry, 2019

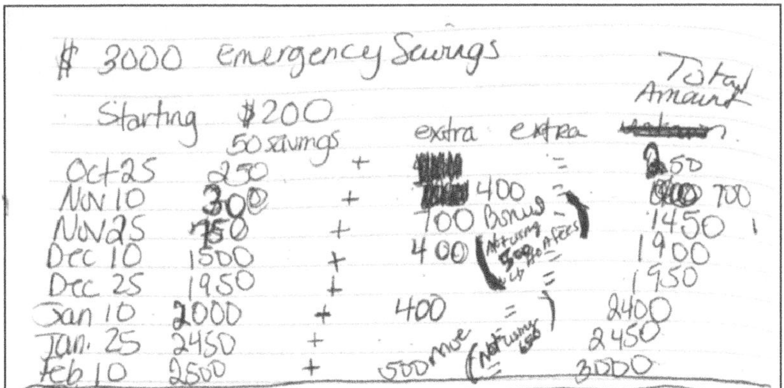

Having even a small emergency fund helped me during the Pandemic. Having one didn't cause the emergencies, but not having one would've exacerbated the emergencies I had. Call this fund whatever you want, but don't forget the power of planning and saving.

This is why we need financial plans such as insurance, emergency funds, retirement accounts, legal services, ridding ourselves of debt, and other protections and policies in place to safeguard our way of life, our mental stability, and our futures. It's easier to avoid jail time for those who have family lawyers or the means to get access to one. Do you get where I'm coming from?

We're either in a crisis or actively living our best life until a crisis hits. Having a contingency plan is a better way to operate than walking around as if our world will never crash.

Whether you're a Believer or not, the very act of Joseph storing up grain saved his family and an entire nation of people.

Write: What's your plan to prepare for the *what if's* in your life? How will you bounce back? How will you pay for them? Who's your go-to person to help you realign and synergize when disaster strikes?

Having an umbrella during a storm doesn't stop you from getting wet. Would you rather have it or not?

We can't plan every detail of our lives, but we can make it easier on ourselves by viewing life through lenses instead of blindfolds.

Instead of letting the ***what-ifs*** dominate your life, put the appropriate policies and strategies in place that will keep you winning and on your path to success.

Habakkuk 2:2: "Write the vision and make it plain."

When I look back on my life, I don't think there is one goal that I did not write down first or keep at the forefront of my mind. If you want to see some good things happen in your life, *hunnie*, write them down! I have been amazed when I go back to read my journals. Inside lies goals, aspirations, dreams, pains, excuses, and answered prayers. It is incredible to read what I was thinking and how I felt at the time. I have witnessed how I charted my way to getting rid of debt on various accounts, laying the ground to fix work problems, or thinking through relationship issues; I wrote them down. The satisfaction you get from seeing one of your goals accomplished is priceless.

Journal Entry, 2013

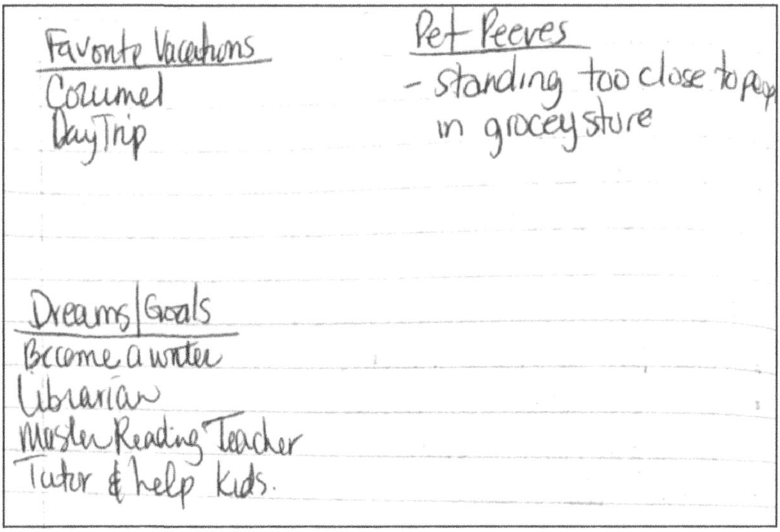
Favorite Vacations
Cozumel
Day Trip

Pet Peeves
- standing too close to peop
in grocey store

Dreams | Goals
Become a writer
Librarian
Master Reading Teacher
Tutor & help kids.

In 2018, I became an Elementary Librarian. You're witnessing the first one!

Write down the salary you want, the job you plan to get, the business you want to start, or the family you wish to have—write the vision first and make it plain, then hopefully, you will stumble across your words in the distant future. If you can think it and pen it down, the likelihood of it coming to pass is that much greater. The possibility of you showing up and doing the work increases. The idea that you dared to dream gives your ambitions power.

Writing is also therapeutic and healing. It can be a form of self-care. It's no wonder that therapists ask many of their clients to reflect using a journal. Sometimes, your journals are the only place you can get out what you're thinking. You can deal with your deepest issues in a judge-free zone.

It's a place to come face-to-face with tragedy and failures, big dreams and curiosities—such an intimate conversation with you and the pages you fill. Writing is one of the most impactful ways to express and heal yourself.

And what heals your soul better than the promises in the Bible? God's Word is written for His people. Impressions of the lives lost during the Holocaust are scribbled and carved on walls, hieroglyphics tell the story of past African culture, and diaries of soldiers and narratives from slaves speak of atrocious acts and glimpses of hope. How important it is to our way of life that we remember historical acts. You need to record your history, so it becomes that much more imperative that you come out victorious. Just think: Why was it so important for the Word to be in script? Why would prisoners of war write and carve their names on walls? Why do cultures adopt written languages in the first place? You see, writing is powerful. We write to preserve our very lives.

We recreate life and historical periods through written works, preserving precious history and dictating our futures with bills and laws signed into existence. The act of writing is so important that at one point, it was only for elitists—scribes. How then, if we, in our finiteness, would put mere words on paper that we would prosper and preserve our very life, simultaneously giving us life beyond reason. The power that you hold by this simple act will define how pressing your ambitions are. It will determine the actuation behind your intentions. And it will justify your habits and actions.

Journal entry 2015

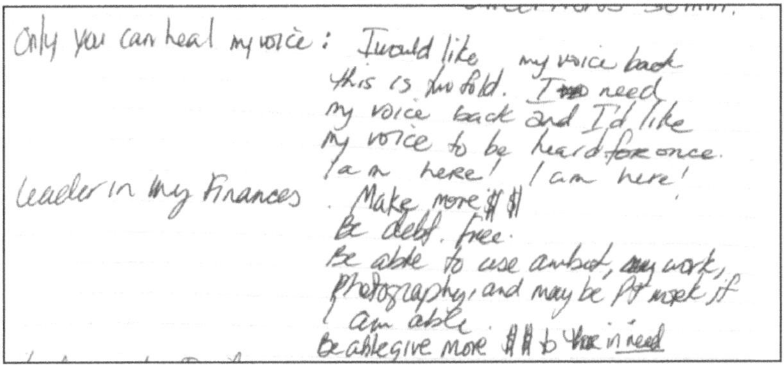
Only you can heal my voice: I would like my voice back this is two fold. I need my voice back and I'd like my voice to be heard for once. I am here! I am here!

Leader in my Finances: Make more $$! Be debt free. Be able to use artwork, my work, photography, and maybe PT work if I am able. Be able give more $$ to those in need

I'm using my voice now. Four years later I started my debt-free journey. #justification

Habakkuk 2:2 (KJV) gives hope in what we should do for our own lives. In a time of trouble and despair, Habakkuk had valid complaints about what was happening before him. His answer was to, "...Write the vision, and make it plain upon tables,...." Though this comes from a Biblical standpoint for God's people and what would happen in the future, we can use it to guide our lives. WRITE! I tell you. Write your vision for your life. Write what happened. Write what is happening. Write what will happen. It may not come all at once, or even in the exact way you hoped or planned, but it will surely come as long as God approves it!

Journal Entry, ~2016

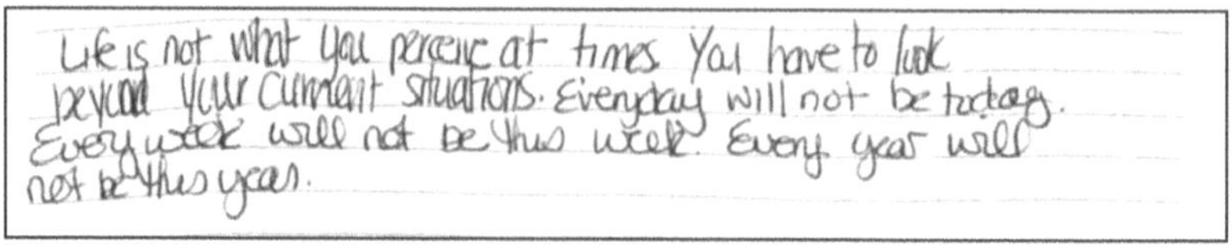
Life is not what you perceive at times. You have to look beyond your current situations. Everyday will not be today. Every week will not be this week. Every year will not be this year.

The hope I found in my writing is truly a blessing.

Start now: Write down your dreams, hopes, disappointments, and goals, then see how perpetuating it will be to your life. When you're ready to get rid of stress, write it down. Ready to win the battle over your finances? Write it down. Ready to walk anew? Write. It. Down. Then take action. Stop here and get to writing—put it all down.

The floor is yours.

Celebrate Small Wins

We agree that it's essential to have something to push forward to in life. If we somehow fail to keep pushing, we will lose ourselves. Our vision will become narrow, and then we become a part of a monotonous cycle of life, which can lead to dark roads (addictions, cheating, negative thinking, spending money on meaningless objects, etc.). Fill your life with purpose, and use your goals to help you fulfill that desire.

Sometimes, however, we fail to realize the small steps it takes for us to get there. We focus so much on the end goal that we may forget to celebrate the small victories and even the hurdles we have to get over to get there. The goal is to chart each step that is needed so you can celebrate on the way up. If you have a minor setback, remind yourself of what you have accomplished. As I built my emergency fund, several obstacles came up, and I wasn't able to contribute as much as I intended, pushing my plans back. Even while writing this book, problem after problem tried to rob me from finishing this book, but every chapter and sub-chapter I finished felt like an enormous hurdle accomplished! Even throughout the editing stages, I got sick and had every reason to stay in bed relaxing, but I figured God gave me this time to finish. I got my tissues, snacks, heater, blankets, medicines, cell phone, and computer and plugged away while quarantined in my room. Thankfully, I tested negative for COVID-19! I even lost water in my home, my car broke down, and I spent nearly $11,000 in emergencies from the time I started this book one year prior. But through it all, I celebrated each stage. "*It could be worse*," I often repeat. I didn't have to add more debt, thank-fully. And you know what? My family and oldest and best friend were there to encourage me! Y'all better get some family and friends like mine! It's contagious. It's a blessing!

Humans like quick gratification, so short and attainable objectives will help you keep sight of your long-term aspirations (those goals).

Whether it's an announcement on social media, blessing someone else, taking a break or time to relax, bingeing on a favorite show, or having an easy kickback at the house, don't forget to celebrate! The possibilities are limitless; however, keeping it small and simple (free or cheap) is always better while you're working through your financial journey. It's a sure way to win and set up a tremendous reward for the end.

> **Side note**: Please, don't go overboard! We want to celebrate to keep our minds focused on the positive, but don't use celebrations as a cop-out to overly spend. We're still trying to decrease our stress and curb bad habits. Keep your eyes on the target.

While you're charting your progress, keep a visual aid. Whether it's a list, a coloring chart, or another tool to help you keep track of how you're progressing, it will keep you pumped and excited. This goes along with writing it down!

Make your vision visible (sticky notes, alerts, etc.) so you keep your eye on targeted ambitions and keep your stress levels down when you have setbacks. Focus on what you completed, and use your accomplished tasks as motivation. It takes effort to see the glass half-full, a lesson in growth mindset (see chapter I). If you need visuals on how to chart your success, go to my bonus materials at bonus.findyourspark.info and use them or get creative and design your own! Either way, shred the stress by acknowledging and reveling in your success.

Write: What small wins have you accomplished recently? Share them with your real squad!

CHAPTER III:

Talk it Out

There comes a time when our silence is betrayal. Our words bring us healing. Proverbs 15:4 tells us, “A wholesome tongue is a tree of life…(KJV).” To benefit from such wisdom, we have to begin to open our mouths to 1. Speak life into our situations. 2. Share our story with others because we try to bear the whole burden of stress alone. Let me tell you: THERE’S NO REWARD IN DOING SO! There are people out there preaching to move silently, don’t tell anyone your moves, or keep it on the down-low. There has been more brokenness for the sake of, “What happens in this house, stays in this house!” We are not created to be in isolation. We are not built to keep silent. Secrecy destroys us from the inside out. And if you’re running in a circle where you can’t tell someone your fears, failures, or future dreams, then you need to find a new crew!

"What happens in this house stays in this house" has broken a lot people and families."

The tree of life is ever giving and yielding seeds, and that's how words can be: an uplifting gift that keeps on giving. In this chapter, I encourage you to speak up about your stressors to others near, far, and unlikely sources.

We will dive into the benefits of discussing your situation, even with some trustworthy strangers. You need real friends, outside support, or support from an expert. The power of hearing the right words, from the right person, at the right time is the difference between life and death. It has the power to hold you back and the power to propel you forward. The power to divert your dreams. The power to help you conquer. Your confidants can help you change the trajectory of your stressful life if and when you learn to talk it out.

"Our lives begin to end the day we become silent about the things that matter."

Dr. Martin Luther King, Jr.

Choose Wisely

There's nothing more stressful than opening up your heart to the wrong person. Imagine telling your deepest, darkest secrets, only for them to be splattered all over the place as rumors and gossip to friends, family, or even coworkers, or worse yet, looked at without regard, no response, or thrown back in your face. Someone right now is saying, *that's why I don't talk to anyone*. It's hard enough that you're already going through the issue, but now it's Community News, falls on deaf ears, or used to abuse and excuse you. Something like this could cause you to have an alarming amount of unhealthy stress and increased anxiety.

Journal Entry, 2015

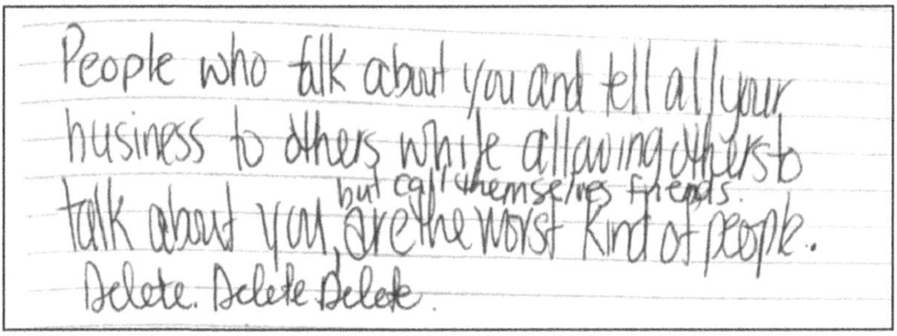
People who talk about you and tell all your
business to others while allowing others to
but call themselves friends.
talk about you, are the worst kind of people.
Delete. Delete Delete.

We have all been through this, but don't let it stop you from crafting quality conversations with quality people.

It is imperative to talk to the right person(s) whenever you feel overwhelmingly stressed; people of quality, like-minded, and of integrity. Being able to release how you feel to someone unbiased, has a listening ear, and even some good and healthy advice will aid you in reducing your stress levels, relaxing your mind, and building more positive experiences. Don't forget about writing it down, too. When you're stressed out, you need some positive vibes coming your way.

It might even help you grow closer to some unlikely God-sent friends.

The freeing feeling you have when you get out of your head and in front of a listening ear is life-changing. Even the Bible tells us to "confess your sins to each other and pray for each other so that you may be healed. The prayer of a righteous person is powerful and effective (James 5:16)." And though it may not be sin that you're confessing, healing is the result. Psalms 32:3 reminds us that "when we keep silent, we waste away." Silence and alone time is always needed, but sometimes our silence continues to accentuate and exacerbate the stress in our lives. Our silence deepens the pain we experience even one step further, keeping us from growth and prosperity.

Discussing your stress is like dumping a truckload of emotional weight. If you're talking to the right person, you should feel lighter because the right person will listen. The right person will make you feel better about yourself (even when they are correcting you). The right person is going to acknowledge what you have to say. And the right person may or may not give you sound advice, meaning they may not choose to say anything but listen—you might need this more than you need advice.

The advice given will come without the expectation that you follow verbatim. It's your life, and they understand that you have to make your own choices. This person understands that you're an individual and that you will make the most appropriate and healthy choices for you. (I hope that you are making healthy choices, but that does not always happen as we go through our journey.) They will not look to admonish you for future decisions, but you're going to get the truth (if it's a true friendship). A circle of quality people is like the roots of a solid tree.

> **Side note:** I say this knowing very much how it feels to be in a relationship with someone who wants control. People who feel some way because you did not take their advice and dare to call you on it and ask you, "*Why ask me questions when you never take my advice*," have a complex. Most people have already decided on what they will do before they even talk to someone else. They usually want someone to listen so that they can say it out loud. Someone who is not out to control you knows that it's your life, your choices, and your consequences at the end of the day. They may say their bit, but one way or another, they know it's all on you. Your *confidant* will love you nonetheless but may exert their boundaries if said choices begin to affect them.

Depending on your relationship, they may check on you or see how you're doing with your situation. Ultimately, your supporter won't be trying to control what you do and how you do it because you have to live with the consequences at the end of the day. When it comes to talking it out, find someone who *truly cares* for you and has mutual respect.

Will talking to someone magically make all your problems go away? No. But you will feel better when you've masterminded with others and dropped some of the weight. How long are you going to carry it around, anyway?

Gaining wisdom from a different perspective, building positive binding relationships, and developing shared experiences will help you along your journey. Here is where you gather the heat source to ignite your spark. Don't be afraid to open your mouth. Or who cares, be frightened and open your mouth anyway. You need the advice and healing that someone else can provide.

I caution you, however, to be mindful. Avoid leaning on others so much that you push them away. Have balance. People are not responsible for your actions, emotions, or situation. Be careful not to project your issues on others or expect them to invite them into their intimate space. In doing so, you allow them to be objective and remain a valuable source to you on your journey. Know that others have their issues as well, and a healthy relationship is a balance between giving and taking, meaning instead of gleaning, listen and give as much as you talk and take.

If most of your stress is bottled up, try to choose wise counsel to help you on your journey. Because when you cross the finish line, there is nothing better than having a team cheering for you on the sidelines—pom-poms and all!

Write: Name some trusted friends or wise confidants you can talk to about your finances and stress. How do you know you can trust them? List their qualities, and use this as an opportunity to thank them for being in your life.

Go Outside Your Bubble: Start Communicating

We've all heard the phrase, "it takes a village," but somehow, we only apply that to raising children. We are social people, and we do all kinds of activities together: we celebrate holidays and memorable moments, worship in our various religious places, build businesses to support our families, entertain friends, dine out, learn in classroom environments, raise money to support causes, protest, pray for one another, rock it out, play video games, heal the sick via a medical team, make movies, write books, and thousands of other activities: **TOGETHER**!

Almost everything we do takes the community to survive. Our entire existence is based on coming together to procreate. We cannot exist alone. We should not exist alone. No matter how "to yourself" you consider yourself to be (*and I love being to myself)*, you are part of a community of people who work to keep your livelihood going. Therefore, when you're trying to get rid of stress and anxiety, finding a support group outside of your norm could be beneficial.

Remember, *we* got ourselves into the problem, so *we* need a new set of eyes, beliefs, and habits to get us out of it. Having someone on the outside gives you great insight into your situation. Quality people who are not in your entanglement (LOL) can often provide excellent clarity, and it takes the pressure off of you.

It's like a vacation because you're leaving all your other baggage at home. The outside world gets only a smidgen of you (not *all* of your problems).You get to focus on specific aspects of your life and get support from a community of less judgmental people. Most importantly, your *outside bubble* will have great advice and, many times, first-hand experience about your predicament. Whether you seek individuals in your established outer circle (like coworkers, distant cousins, church group, etc.) or a new group of "*like-troubled*" people to chop it up with, you'll be doing yourself a huge favor.

For instance, social media groups are easily accessible places to gain new friends, which can be very informative and self-soothing. When I was going through a stressful period learning about narcissistic personality disorder (NPD), I joined a group that discussed this one topic. The wealth of knowledge I received from the group was helpful. I learned so much information that each time I read posts or engaged in conversations, I became more aware of what I had experienced. The irony is that running toward your pain is what will heal you. I would've kept every word to myself in the past, but this outside community was a rare jewel.

Groups provide you with a chance to meet people who have healed, are currently in the storm, are hurting, are in denial, and those determined to get out of their dilemma. In my NPD community, I was able to encourage others, I was able to be inspired, and I was able to sit back and witness others' experiences. And because it was an online community of strangers brought together by a unique set of circumstances, I was able to be in a non-threatening and freeing environment—the ability to be myself, without judgment (go figure), and dip in and out of conversations as I saw fit.

The people who love you the most will not always be the ones who can help you out of your stressful condition. Jesus always left the group to pray and examine his path (*I suggest you do this too!*). What will you do?

A cloudy mind makes for illogical and inadequate decisions.

You may not bear your whole soul online (and I caution you not to), but don't miss out on the positive interactions you can have with people within social media groups or groups in your local community. The fact that you have instant access is even better when you're up late and your stress takes over the hours you should be sleeping.

The point here is to find quality people to be around so that you can cultivate healthy habits, discussions, and goals! The energy you get when you find quality people is amazing. These relationships will hold you accountable and help you move forward in your journey. The coworkers I reached out to helped me considerably when I was going through a difficult time.

Remember: You can't get new results with old habits. Consider this: the people you've entertained are not the solution to your problem. Take a chance! Get to know some "outsiders" that you may already know but have spent very little time nurturing the relationship.

A final word about outside communities is that you should use your discernment while chartering into new territories. We all have opinions, and not everyone's opinion on what you should do will be valid for you. Everything is not for you, but don't discount solid advice, either. Gather strength from the circles you create.

"*Alone, we can do so little; together, we can do so much.*"
Helen Keller

Ask for Support

I need your help! How often do we say this? If you're like me, raised from cast-iron strength, bred latchkey kid, then you rarely use these words in your personal life. We may have to say it at work depending on the position we hold, but many of us take pride in fixing things ourselves, doing the work on our own, accomplishing tasks to inflate our chests, just a bit. Right?

We could be drowning in debt, overworked, or in an actual life-threatening situation and still miss proclaiming the few little words that could give us a few extra lives or a few deep breaths when it comes to winning the game of life. We need that self-defining title: I did that! SMH.

Why do we feel so much shame when we ask for help? Who taught us that? Where did we learn that? And why are we holding on to it?

Unfortunately, some of us may have had authorities in our lives who told us to figure it out, shunned, talked about, straight up clowned or accused when asking for aid, or even given the run around when our supervisors or trainers wanted to teach us a lesson. Let's face it: many of us have been publicly and privately shamed for simply asking for help or asking questions in general. In other words, we have been trained to equate asking for help with negativity because of our experiences.

It's discouraging, especially from *so-called* leaders.

Heck, I'm tired of dragging myself through the mud before I ask for help. It's time to speak up and ask for support that sometimes I desperately need. And whether I get it or not, I asked (the right person, hopefully). The goal is to ask, so I put in the proper practice to remove barriers in my life.

What about you? Will you release the "*I can do it all by myself!*" banner? Or will you be too ashamed or prideful to ask for help when you get in a bind?

We all know the saying, "a closed mouth doesn't get fed." So, please don't be ashamed to speak up and ask for help. You may have to take it for a test run at first; however, the more you say these words when in need, the more you invite your family, friends, and coworkers into your world. It takes humility and strength to ask for assistance, but we all need some support during our lifetime. Don't fall into the American Individualism hype; we win together!

Think about it: How would you feel if you asked for support and received it? Great, right? And if you didn't, what did you lose? Nothing!

You probably have people in your corner who will let you talk to them if you tell them that you need to vent without guilt, shame, or advice. You could say: "*I need your help. Do you mind if I talk to you about an issue I'm stressing about? I'm having a hard time and need someone to listen to me. Can you keep it between you and me*?" That's a start.

It may seem juvenile to put those words on your lips, but think how often we refuse to ask for what we need. Don't be that person who supports every homie from your *hood*, family member, charity or fundraiser, job initiative, significant other, and NOT yourself.

Say the words. No matter how much of a boss you are, say the words: *I need help*.

You have needs, too. Your mindfulness about your financial, mental, physical, or spiritual health is just as important as the people and organizations you love. Note that support is not always monetary. There are other ways for people to show up in your life, so I urge you to keep an open mind.

If you're not comfortable ***yet***, or maybe the environment you're in is not a positive conduit, then find the right people or organizations to ask for help. (skip to Chapter IV: Choose Your Circle Carefully). Remember, it's okay to go outside your bubble! And feel free to jump into our private online community at group.findyourspark.info to find support from others; social media is a great place to get answers and ask for help in various ways.

> **Write**: List people in each area of your life that you could connect with and ask for support when needed. List their skills and characteristics that might be helpful to you. For example, some people are great listeners while others are not. Choose wisely.

Be Honest

When we are telling our tales, we tend to make ourselves the protagonist of our plot twist. We adore the *ahhs* and the *ooos* so much that we develop "yes'm" characters in our lives—people who agree with everything we say, one hundred percent. Such people have nothing to offer you. You will never get out of *Stressville* if you keep dishonest people around you. While they may have great intentions, the fake smiles, the fake feedback, and the fake happiness are detrimental to your growth. A tree is only as good as the soil it's in, and no matter how much rain and sun it gets, if it's rooted in shallowness (dishonesty), it won't stand for long. Make sure you keep honesty in your core values. Demand honesty from others around you, and plant your feet in it for your life.

Listen, if you're trying to move out of your situation, be authentic so that you can receive objective feedback. You get out what you put in. If you throw out lies, you're going to get fake feedback, fake advice and star in a fake production of your life.

"*See what had happened was....*" So you played the villain in your story. It's okay. Your circle of quality persons of influence *got* you. Make your omission so that you can move forward. You're guilty.

Ouch!

That hurts, but it's healthy. You are simply revealing areas in which you probably could have made some different decisions. You're not always going to get it right, but have that conversation in a safe environment: fess up. If I hadn't gotten this finance stuff and stress stuff so wrong, I couldn't possibly be talking about it now. You have to go through some tough times to build a pillar to stand on. And it would help if you had quality people who will listen, hold you accountable, and then move you forward.

On the other hand, sometimes our distress comes from actions we have refused to undertake, neglected tasks, or credible advice we rejected. Whatever the reason, be truthful about your participation in your current state. But be careful not to mull over these mistakes or intentional decisions with great effort. Lingering over what you should've done will only leave your mind muddled with increased anxiety. Let it out, pout if you need to, say your apologies or make it right, and then take precise action towards your goals.

On the real: You don't have to admit everything to everyone. Write it down (talk to the Man upstairs, we say). Be honest with yourself first, and then have that conversation in a group of trusting people, whether with a professional, a close and trustworthy friend, or a group of caring individuals, when you're ready. In the end, your conversations will begin to calm the raging waters in your heart, for "the tongue has the power of life and death (Proverbs 18:21 NIV)."

Write: Name three things that you need to be brutally honest about and make a plan to keep it to yourself or discuss it with someone trustworthy. What will it cost you to keep it to yourself or divulge this information to someone?

Go Pro!

There comes a time when the world is unraveling around you, and you have no control. When you get to a place where everything in your life is out of control, and internally, you're on fire, you can't get a breath of air because you feel like you're drowning, and you can't manage life on your own, seek help! You might be having anxiety or a panic attack!

And then there are other times in life that recurring experiences take place, or you're attracting the same circumstances or people, or there may be a nagging habit you can't seem to tame. Again, seek professional help. We try so hard to complete tasks on our own. We congratulate ourselves on getting to the finish line. We brush off.our shoulders with the thought that, " I, alone, did that!"

Is your success better than someone who got the help you didn't seek? Don't get me wrong: It's great that anyone can pull themselves out of darkness—and sometimes we have to go at it alone, but there are many times we don't, being that others are within reach. What's stopping people from going to seek help? Is it shame, guilt, or pride? It's wrapped up in all of these emotional states. However, you don't get any more accolades than the next king or queen who was able to get out of their dark corners of the world. You healed or dealt with your situation, and that's all that matters.

Journal Entry, 2015

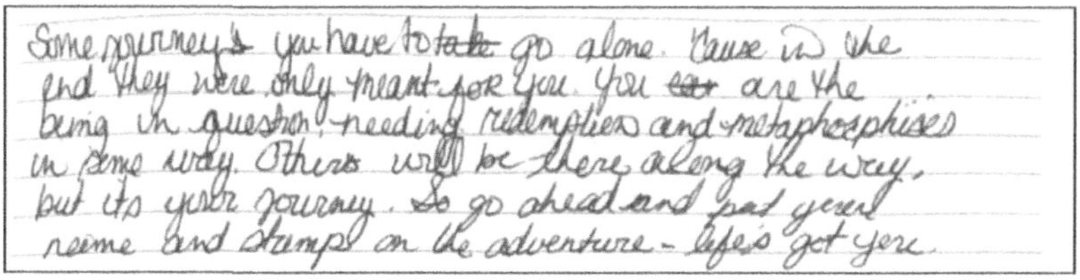
Some journey's you have to ~~take~~ go alone. 'Cause in the end they were only meant for you. You ~~can~~ are the being in question, needing redemption and metaphosphises in some way. Others will be there along the way, but its your journey. So go ahead and put your name and stamps on the adventure - life's got you.

Emphasis on "sometimes". Only if I had reached out earlier, journal entries like this would be few and far in between. Being a lone in your mess keeps you stagnant longer than needed at times.

There comes a time when some of us need help from a professional, like a counselor or psychologist. Counseling will challenge you. And sometimes, we need to be challenged and not coddled. One will keep you where you are, and the other will push you out of your comfort zone. If you want to grow further than you've imagined, elicit the help of a professional therapist. Find someone just right for you. Therapists are not one size fits all, so make sure you get with someone you feel you can trust and help you on your journey. When you figure out that process, let me know. Finding the right fit can be challenging, but you'll know when it happens. So, while they're interviewing you, you should be interviewing them, too. You're sharing the most sacred part of you, so why not? I always like to ask for recommendations from trusted friends, church leaders, or your doctor.

If you're not sure whether you should talk with someone, that may be the actual reason you should seek help because it's already percolating in your mind. Here are a few tips to help recognize if and when you or someone you know should seek a mental health professional:

1. You are life-threatening to yourself or others.
2. You're overwhelmed and can't seem to get back to doing life.
3. Daily and routine functions have become mountainous tasks, causing you to act differently at home, school, or work.
4. You can't seem to bounce back from a difficult or traumatic situation.
5. Your behavior or emotional well-being is erratic.
6. Others are starting to worry about you, but nothing they do seems to help.
7. You are not attending to your physical or emotional needs (no self-care).
8. You're withdrawn from others for extensive amounts of time (abnormal behavior) or having difficulty in your relationships.

9. You continuously harbor, replay, and act out negative scenarios or experiences in your head.
10. You use other substances or have detrimental coping habits.

There are so many signs that point to seeking the help of a mental health professional, but often, we avoid doing the obvious. Going pro will help you find and flame the sparks that are within you. It's about getting on the right track for your life.

I'm not a mental health provider, but I have seen how financial stress can break people down: flat-out anxiety attacks, strokes, and even paranoia. I've talked with people and been in rooms where people have admitted that their financial stress is so great that it caused them to have a heart attack. The rate of suicide rises as people are overwhelmed financially. I worked as an intake coordinator for a mental health company. I can tell you the devastation that money elicits is life and death. I've been privileged to listen to patients discuss how their marriage has ended in divorce, spouses committing suicide, depression, and homelessness because of financially stressed circumstances. After witnessing someone give up their children because of financial stress, I can only empathize and continue to spread the message of economic power and stability. Taking care of our personal economies must take center stage.

Such tragedies are why I focus on getting the mind right and the stress under control before you attempt to tackle the total weight of your finances.

Seeking help from mental health professionals is not a *white thing*, but the right decision for your life when you need it. It's about giving life to dry bones, making the invisible visible, and conquering the spiritual warfares we battle.

If you don't take care of yourself, who will? Not even a spouse, a parent, or a friend can do the mental work for you. You have to know that you are worth it. You have to know that you need it. You have to know that counseling does not take anything away from you. Get the help you need so you can get back on your throne. Talk it out so you can walk it out! I need you to thrive and move into your excellence.

If you need help but are a bit shy, or maybe you lack the resources, go to the bonus.findyourspark.info site.

LISTEN as Much as You Talk

Listening in the talking section? Yes ma'am! Yes sir! It's the gateway to learning. It's how you know everything you know and believe—even if you read it in a book. You still had to *listen* to the information. Here is where you need to tame your venting so you can be open to hear what your encouragers have to say. It could be a bit much if all you ever did were to talk about *your* stressful circumstances. How long do you think that will last before you or another person is exhausted? Taking and never giving, well, that's not right! So listening is where we give back.

Show people that you're listening by:

1. Eliminating distractions (avoid cell phones, television, games, etc.)
2. Lean in and posture yourself to hear what they have to say.
3. Shhh! Just listen. You don't always have to say something.

4. Shhh, 2.0! Opt-out of giving advice when you know you're not the best person to offer an answer.
5. Ask questions based on their conversation. Instead of chiming in to get your point in there, ask more questions to help understand their situation or the advice they may be giving you.
6. Be genuine. Ooh, enough said. Be honest. Be real. Don't sugarcoat.
7. When they are looking for you to speak or asking for an answer, repeat or rephrase what they said to show you were listening.
8. If they are dropping some tea you already know, it's OK to drop a few, "*for real, girl/man get out, stop, you playing, I can't with you*," and keep it moving (lol)!

Y'all needed this, right? Or are you too grown? I know plenty of adults who don't know how to listen and take, take, and take! No one wants to be in a one-sided relationship. Make sure you're a good listener. Otherwise, relearn the necessary skills needed to connect with others.

Feeling connected to others is critical in a conversation. We make people feel important and supported when we listen. And it's FREE! IT'S FREE to lend an ear! It makes us feel good when our boss, significant other, children, students, friends, or family listens. Then flip that notion to understand how you will feel when something *you* say has a positive impact. Pure bliss!

We not only give to our supportive community when we listen, but we also give to ourselves. We give ourselves permission to be counseled and learn new information that we can utilize for personal gains. We permit ourselves to dismiss the opinions of others that we deem are not in line with our path to healing and winning in life.

Take note that your battle with stress will be more triumphant when you lean into others more than you lean into your thoughts and self-proclivities. Be steadfast and attentive to listen with your mind and heart. Listening is the superpower we tend to overlook. Do more than nod your head; lean forward and mend your mind.

Write: Who was the last person you listened to? How can you improve your listening skills?

CHAPTER IV:

Temptations—The Pebbles in Your Shoe

When we focus our eyes on the hills ahead we blur out the details in front of us. Naturally, we think it's the big issues in our lives that keep us down. We don't make enough money, our job is the problem, or we don't have enough education, or if only we could get rid of this person in our life everything would be okay. There could be some merit to each of those issues; however, we could accomplish each one and still end up back where we started. In order for change, you have to change: your mind and your habits. Your gaze has to shift to see the minute details and actions you need to take now. It's usually not the monumental things that break us down, it's the tiny pebbles that collect in our shoes. They show up in our lives in various ways as we walk this world—a missed payment, a late fee, someone borrowing money, shopping to keep up at work, saying yes when we should've said no, charging a few items on our credit cards, etc.). Oh, how harmless they all seem.

However, at some point the collection of pebbles makes it unbearable to walk. Same as our decisions—they start adding up, become stressful, and cause major problems in our lives. Our temptations are the small details we need to pay attention to. We have to execute a strategy to avoid them, refocus our minds, choose the right people to be around, and cut where necessary.

You are going to be challenged in this chapter to make some major changes—changes that will alter your life should you take action. These changes will make you uncomfortable. However, you must strategically put yourself in uncomfortable situations that will stretch you if you want to grow. The refining process is ugly; a diamond must undergo some added pressure. The welder creates amazing structures by hammering and putting metal in the fire. Put yourself in the fire and work on the minutiae of everyday life which keep you in turmoil.

"It isn't the mountains ahead that tear you down. It's the pebble in your shoe."
Muhammad Ali

Limit Access to Stressful Situations

Some people may think that limiting stressful situations sounds like a no-brainer, right? Why would anyone put themselves in a stressful situation in the first place? Often, we don't look at the little contrivances that get in the way of our success. It's the minute habits and people in our daily lives that drive a wedge between us and our goals: cooking instead of eating out, listening to positive discussions instead of hoarding gossip, saying *no* to a friend instead of going into a toxic environment, holding our tongue (conserving our energy) instead of inciting an argument. Small changes in your choices lead to your treasure. It's not as easy as it sounds because you need to do *the thinking* before *the doing*.

People don't always think about putting themselves in stressful situations until they're face to face and knee-deep in it. We're incredibly reflective after the fact, and our most prominent question is *why*. We have to be mindful and metic-ulous not to put ourselves in specific conversations around certain people, go to certain places, browse or shop specific sites, subscribe to certain listings, or say certain things.

If you're not proactive about what you feed your senses (sight, sound, taste, smell, and touch), you'll set yourself up for failure. Until you're strong enough not to buy that purse, put that cookie in your mouth, get angry from what your adversary has said, or run off at the mouth, you have to cut off access to anything robbing you of your joy.

There are tasks we can control, but controlling people is not one of them. Limit what you can to deal with life on better terms. You need to find your peace and have equilibrium to get to the place where you can breathe, think, plan, and dominate your habits. Turn off the tv, get the gossip out of your life, hide or delete people and things from your social media timeline, unsubscribe from lists and people trying to take your money and tranquility, and leave. Then subscribe to people and items that lift your spirits, nurture your soul and mind, and give you practical habits. Spend the least amount of time with the stressor(s) if possible. If it's a person you live with, that's hard. Try to avoid arguments that drain you (protect your emotional energy). Limit your conversations with stressful people outside your home. You have got to run from these things when you are deep-sea diving in Stressville.

It's tempting to keep yourself open to everyone and everything in your life, but it will harm you more than help. We must learn to put up roadblocks and security locks to parts of our life. Your life will look different when you start to limit access to what people, objects, and activities get from you. Limit access to your time, money, and listening ear. I believe this to be one of the keys to eliminating stress and moving toward your financial breakthrough.

Write: Make a list of what tempts you. Decide which temptations add stress to your life. Make a plan: how can you limit the temptations? Journal why you are tempted and how your temptations add stress to your life. How does it make you feel?

<table>
<tr><th>My Temptations</th><th>Stress Level
☆ - low to
☆☆☆☆ - high</th><th>What can I do about it?</th></tr>
<tr><td>Christmas shopping</td><td>☆☆☆☆</td><td>Buy presents for kids only. Start a Setup a Christmas fund all year.</td></tr>
<tr><td colspan="3">Journal writing: I like to buy presents for people during this time because it makes me feel joyful. But it's stressful because I don't always have the money to pay for everyone's gifts. I usually have to cross names off my list or I'll spend on my credit card. It takes me a long time to pay off these things, and I usually don't have anything left in savings.</td></tr>
<tr><td>Eating out</td><td>☆</td><td>Budget an amount. Fast from eating out. Use gift cards to limit spending. Plan meals and cook!</td></tr>
<tr><td colspan="3">Journal writing: Cooking is annoying. LOL! Especially, when I'm one person. I like eating out. It's easy, quick, and I can get back to working. It saves time, but it costs me a lot. Eating out doesn't stress me, cooking does! But I could save $$$ if I cooked more.</td></tr>
</table>

An example of what you could put in your journal!

Redirect Your Focus

How relaxing would it be to escape your problems for some time? We can take a 40-day retreat as Jesus did, maybe not in the wilderness. But notice how He used his time away—in preparation, focusing, and restructuring where His thoughts and energy would go in spite of the persistent temptation. So I am asking you to do the same.

We can't always escape physically, so we have to be a bit more creative. I'm suggesting that you get a hobby. Get a project. Redirect your focus. Do something that will help you *run away* while you are in the midst and height of your stress.

We have to do things that help us govern our lives—take back control. Your project will allow you to do that and avoid temptations like thinking or talking negatively, shopping and spending money irresponsibly, and put a halt to moping around being unproductive.

Choose something that is enriching and helps you to be the best version of yourself. You may choose to volunteer at a food bank, or learn a new skill like sewing, self-defense, kickboxing, weightlifting, or learning about stock trading, gardening, cake decorating, joining a book club, training for a marathon, fostering a pet, volunteering at a homeless shelter, or assisting teachers at your child's school. The choices are limitless. Whatever it is, make it a new and yummy experience so you'll enjoy it and stick to it. The goal is to enrich your life and maybe even others around you. Try taking the focus off you to help someone else and simultane-ously improve your life.

I used my baking skills to get through a tumultuous time in my life and to help me crush debt (Strategy people! Find me at @ginscookies on social media. I was trying to bounce back from awful work experiences, dating experiences, and a relationship in which I learned all about narcissistic personality disorder. In other words, I was doing life!

My mind was all over the place, but I had been in such turmoil for so many years. I stopped holding on to despair and mulling over stressful situations. I made a plan to bake every weekend, work on recipes, and donate my cookies to specific people for feedback (the intro to www.GinsCookies.com.

Since I worked Monday through Friday, I had forty-eight hours to ponder over all the stressful things that were going on in my mind during the weekend. Being single ain't easy, y'all, because we have way too much time to ourselves. To keep cynicism at bay, I baked as an escape. It kept me busy and kept my supporters smiling! I was able to counter and channel the gloom of breakups, loss, and failure into something deliciously sweet. I spent more time planning and thinking about positive outcomes. It gave me a reason to avoid tempting calls, send unneeded texts, and waste time scrolling social media. It refocused my energy every weekend, and my coworkers, friends, and family were thrilled.

People began buying early on during my weekly recipe sprees, so by the summer, I gave my baking a name and a website domain at www.ginscookies.com. The feedback and my recent evaluation of my finances started me on my journey to financial freedom.

When I was baking, I wasn't thinking about my problems. My focus was on making the best recipe for my customer that weekend. I also wasn't feeding into the negativity. I was developing my skills and having fun!!! The peace I had waking up early in the morning, filling my house with sweet aromas, and watching my family and coworkers taste test was a better use of my time and energy.

I wasn't sure exactly where I would end up in the beginning. You never know where the journey will take you and the people you will meet when you take your focus off of your situation and refocus your light on others. (And now I've dedicated my baking to paying off debt.) If you spend too much time recycling negative thoughts and investing in negative energy, do something else with your time: find an escape plan and have some of the best moments in your life!

It will be tempting to do nothing, but those are the times you need to push through. Redirecting your energy and focus will help you decrease stress.

Hopefully, you will find so much joy in your new task(s) that you won't want to quit. When you bring smiles to others, you piece yourself back together little by little until you've reached a place you never knew was attainable.

Write: What hobbies, skills, or volunteer projects could you take up to redirect your energy?

Choose Your Circle Carefully

It's tempting to stay put and keep the same surroundings. But to flourish, we can't let old habits and relationships get in the way of our happiness. If you want to ditch the stress, place yourself in your desired goal. If you want peace, go to a peaceful place. If you want to be a successful business owner, network and commune with other successful business owners. If you wish to have better finances, spend more time with people who have responsible money habits. If you need help with finances, hire financial experts. If you want God in your life, you have to commune with Him daily and surround yourself with others who seek the same. You have to surround yourself with like-minded people.

There is no way to obtain success while dealing with negative family, friends, or coworkers in your ear every day. You need to see, hear, smell, taste, and touch what you're looking for in others. Do you want less stress? Get around some positive people. See what they are doing. Listen to the words they speak to you and the people around them. Smell the aroma of good, positive vibes. And embrace the gentle touches from positive men and women in your life. *Baby*, there is nothing like an excellent source of goodness from optimistic people to entertain your soul.

You will be refreshed and nourished by spending more time with people who want to see you win. People who congratulate you. Who cheers for the minor accomplishments. People who won't let you give up or give in. It is such an euphoric feeling that you won't want to be around anything less. This kind of self-care will sever your relationship with toxic people.

At some point, you will realize the bar you have set. You'll enjoy being in this zone, and any unnecessary interruptions are up for removal. Because once you have witnessed the power of a positive mindset, your stress levels go down, you will feel empowered, and you will protect it at all costs. Find these people in your life! Network with them. Join them. If they don't exist in your immediate circle, create a new circle. Think about joining business networks and or social organizations in person and online. It's a crucial step in ditching the stress you have and moving toward a more fiscal lifestyle.

Write: What negative energies (people or places) are you tolerating in your life? What are you going to do about it? How can you work through it or remove it? What conversations do you need to have, and what do you need to do to move towards more positive environments and relationships with yourself and others? Remember: be honest.

Shape Your Timeline!

Most of us are on social media in some fashion. A place where it's easy to invite all of the negativity and stress into our lives daily. Watching politics, seeing brutality, browsing ads, watching other's achievements, and debating concepts or ideas gets overwhelming and inadvertently stressful! Do it for the 'gram!

These may not seem like stressful situations, but it's the small pebbles that cause an interruption in our lives. The subliminal messages we feed ourselves and the comparisons we secretly subscribe to are destructive. Social media is addictive and damaging to our psyche. We have to protect ourselves by shaping what we are subscribing to each day.

So many people compete with who and what they see online. However, we should not get caught up in the falsetto of faux acts and appearances. There are trolls, advertisements for days, and people posting their best lives and lies. Be aware of it all, and if it's not serving you and your goals, the task is simple: delete, hide, unlike, unfollow, snooze, or block.

You can shape your social media feed to be more impactful. If you have a spending problem, unfollow your favorite brands and stop letting those images pop up in your feed. Delete and unsubscribe from advertising pages that want your money or contact information. Hide or snooze people on your timeline. Delete negative images, pages, and people from your social media. Leave groups that are full of drama.

Once you remove all the things that cause negativity, which fuels stress and incites you to spend, you can start adding affirmation pages, positive messages, and persons who add value to your life. I promise you; it's like a breath of fresh air. If negativity pops up on my timeline, I scroll through that person's timeline. And if they aren't talking about anything progressive, I delete them. I encourage you to follow memes that give you a word of encouragement. Look at timelines that are full of positive vibes. Follow inspirational influencers and motivational speakers. Join debt-free communities and financial groups to surround yourself with a like-minded tribe.

Because social media plays such a dominant role in many of our lives, we have to tame it. We can transform it to be an influential network of impactful and enlightening content. Reshape it to meet your needs. You can only give what you have received. If you only indulge in provocative and hateful content what do you expect to regurgitate? It is counterproductive to download and invite misaligned content into your most private space. Let's be productive by unplugging from harmful social media input and turning on desirable content that favors our goals: becoming stress-free and debt-free.

Scroll your timeline and email: Unsubscribe to pages, ads, or subscriptions that are counterproductive. What inspirational pages can you add? Try searching for: motivation, inspiration, and other positive messages. Look up motivational hashtags (#motivationmonday) and follow them.

BURN THE BRIDGE and the Paths that Lead to It

Skip this sub-chapter! If you didn't come to work, then this is NOT the chapter for you! You're not going to like it, nor will most people do it; it's hard because it has the possibility of leaving you to your own accord, feelings of discouragement, aloofness, in despair, enlightened, relieved, unstressed, and lighter. The concept is a bit oxymoronic, but it will.

I'm going to say it, and you need to hear it:

CUT TOXIC

HABITS,
FAMILY MEMBERS,
FRIENDS,
ORGANIZATIONS,
PEOPLE,
RELATIONSHIPS,
SYSTEMS,
AND WAYS,

OUT OF YOUR LIFE!

It seems extreme, eh? This is the hardest act to execute because we become addicted to toxic people and toxic habits (*look up trauma bonding*). Some of those toxic people live with you. You may be married to them. They could be a parent or an adult child, a family member, a life-long friend, a current or ex-boyfriend or girlfriend, or a boss. Even so, you will need to cut them out of your life, or at least at first, mentally.

> **Side note:** This is NOT a petition to go physically hurt someone...lol! I had to say that! Y'all lighten up.

As I was saying...

What is your sanity and peace worth to you? Who is most important when it comes to your self-care? Them, or your survival?

In my younger years, a boyfriend (who was emotionally and verbally abusive) once told me that if he was the reason for my sadness, "*I should leave him and never let anyone harm me in any such way. Just walk away.*" Why didn't I take the warning?

People know what they are capable of, and sometimes, they will give you a fair warning. Take good notes.

It didn't happen immediately, but eventually, I had to let go. In doing so, I thrived on my own accord. But for a long time, I was bound to this person who wasn't good for me at all. You have to know when to let go of some things, people, and relationships. People will drop small gems in your life about who they are and their capabilities, but they may never remove themselves from your presence. You then have to be the person to say enough is enough.

There's a small window of respect from the toxic person when you disconnect and finally stand up for yourself.

As you remove yourself from people and environments, expect the consequences of such (i.e., loss of financial support, emotional support, relationship loss, fewer friends, feeling lonely, less time with your kids due to custody battles, etc.). It will cost you something, but the other side of the rainbow—the side that's hidden behind the clouds —is so much prettier.

You may feel regret for disengaging, but I urge you to save yourself first. Acknowledge your toxic traits (i.e., low self-esteem/worth/advocacy, trying to be perfect, people-pleasing) that allowed such a relationship to occur. What did you say? What didn't you say? What did you allow? What didn't you allow? When did you open up your mouth to say "*No,*" or "*I don't like it when you...*" or "*You're invading my peace,*" or "*If you do this, then...*" or "*I will not tolerate...*"?

Have those honest conversations with yourself. You will probably find that if you had taken your well-being more seriously and put your health or wealth first, your experience would be profoundly different.

> October 19, 2018 at 10:29 AM
>
> I'm willing to let ppl go if I know it will be the betterment of their well being. That's where I'm at.

I failed to say and my betterment too!

Can you imagine what it would look like if you established healthy boundaries from the beginning?

Ahhh! There's the word we're looking for: **Boundaries**! (#mylovelanguage) Setting down your foot and setting restrictions on how YOU are treated. If you don't train people how to treat you, people will walk all over you in every form: spiritually, physically, sexually, verbally, emotionally, and financially. If there is one takeaway from this book, this is it! My breakthrough matriculated when I **enforced** my boundaries.

When I found my voice and started speaking up for myself, I was so surprised at how easy it was. I was like, "*Well dang, why haven't I done this before?*" It's still a struggle for me at times, but the more you exercise and flex your voice in this area, the more positive relationships you'll have, and that STRESS LEVEL will go DOWN! It's a life-changer, y'all!

Still, without too much delay, remove yourself so that you can focus. We can't instantly get away from everyone, so remove the emotional roller coaster you offer to toxic people each time you interact. You have to get to a point where they cannot upset you.

Know thy enemy.

You must stay one step ahead and take complete control of your reactions. Toxic people and habits cause added stress. You cannot effectively deal with your issues if you refuse to change your harmful traits. (Ooh, catch-22: what if *you're* the toxic person?). Some of your behaviors may even be the cause of your intense situation (e.g. people pleasing, perfectionism, anger issues, avoiding conflict, emotionally unavailable).

In addition, unhealthy environments create cloudy minds and distractions. You must run from the temptation that toxic and damaging people provide. Toxic environments are tempting as they provide us with a false sense of comfort and happiness meanwhile tearing down our very essence. It's a faux existence that will keep you bogged down in *Stressville*, and you'll stay in eternal internal debt. It zaps your energy. You fail to dream, and you remain in a cyclical battle that could end in tragedy.

Think about the movie *Precious* and the negative environment that surrounded her. To give her son a thriving life, she first had to believe in herself, crave more out of life, and then leave. Seriously, how can you prosper if you never take flight–mentally and physically?

Sometimes, we leave too late, and there are permanent damages done, like in the movie *Precious*. PERMANENT scars, y'all. But she still picked herself up and left for the betterment of her child's future. You have to be strong to take the first steps and cut the ties with toxic conditions.

If you feel you can't cut people out of your life, significantly reduce the time you spend with them, or control your emotions around them, so you can avoid pitfalls in your life. However, real talk: We all have the ability; we just aren't prepared for the aftermath. Your decision to cut certain players in the game of life or not *will* cost you. BELIEVE that!

Dancing around the edge of the cliff with your eyes closed and expecting a miracle is a tragedy. Don't expect anything less than the outcome when you knew the end was near.

Side note: You need a good dose of time away from toxicity to gather your composure and strength. It may be forever, a season, or temporary, but no one can deny the power and clarity they gain by removing themselves from negative circumstances.

Think & Write: What boundaries do you need to set in your life? How will you **enforce** them?

Each person's battle in this area will be different. But each of us has to break ties with negativity. And when you do, your life will begin to change in ways you cannot imagine. You will think differently, feel empowered, aspire to greatness, even shed weight (both physically and mentally), and add years back to your life. The outcomes are limitless. Once you remove the dark clouds from over your head, you will glow in a whole new light. Your financial issues have a greater chance of being resolved along with other problems you're experiencing.

Toxicity comes in all shapes and sizes. It could be someone gossiping in your ear every day, verbal abuse, manipulation, emotional abuse, threats or slick jokes, silent treatments, failure to let you express your opinion, and so on. In whatever form it may present itself, find the problem, and gut it out of your life. No one, and I mean no one, will take care of your inner being, self-worth, and self-esteem like you. That's 100% on you.

Give yourself a chance to thrive and burn the bridges of toxicity within yourself, from others, and the paths that lead them to you in the first place. This way, you can avoid repetitive scenarios in your life that keep you from winning and being the ultimate version that my God meant for you.

Brainstorm the toxic habits you are tolerating from yourself and others. What bridges do you need to burn or repair? What will it cost you to keep these relationships in your life? What will it cost you to cut these relationships in your life? How will you sever or repair the relationship? List the steps you need to take. Are you prepared to do what it takes? **Note**: If these are overwhelming and cause too much anxiety, you may need professional help. But you have to do the work to get the results you say you want. Do the work!

CHAPTER V:

Straighten Your Crown and Take Control!

Winning the battle before the battle takes sacrifice, grit, and grace! There are some steps you must commit to before you can put your crown on straight. Kings and Queens take action, then take control!

I admire the salutation, but the daily grind is what roots you in success. What do you think about when you hear King? Queen? If it's eating dainty pastries and basking in royal baths while ignoring the outside world, your vision is skewed. From the images and text that I've been immersed in, Kings and Queens had to make tough decisions, be precise about who was part of the king's court, be knowledgeable about what was happening within their kingdom, and take control by delegating tasks to key persons. It required work. Yes, there are upside benefits, but it was not all sugary treats. If you have to decide if someone lives or dies or take up arms in battle, you might be deterred from being a King and Queen. It's not a statement of beauty; you need to make tough decisions, exposing your true nature. Do we have what it takes to really be a king, a queen? If you want to be *kingly* then you need to straighten your crown–tighten up your personal economies (mindset, health, and wealth), and **get**. **to**. **work**.

Mental work is real--You must get rid of negative thoughts, you must say *no* often, you must get organized, and you must be adamant and orchestrate every dollar that lands in your possession. Proverbs 21:5 guides us, explaining that, “The plans of the diligent lead to profit as surely as haste leads to poverty.”

Successful people don't harvest negativity. They use discernment and know when to say *yes* and *no.* They have an organizational structure. And they manage their money properly.

It’s time to join spaces which allow us to walk a path well worth king and queen status. So, straighten your crown, take *all* your power back, and step into your season!

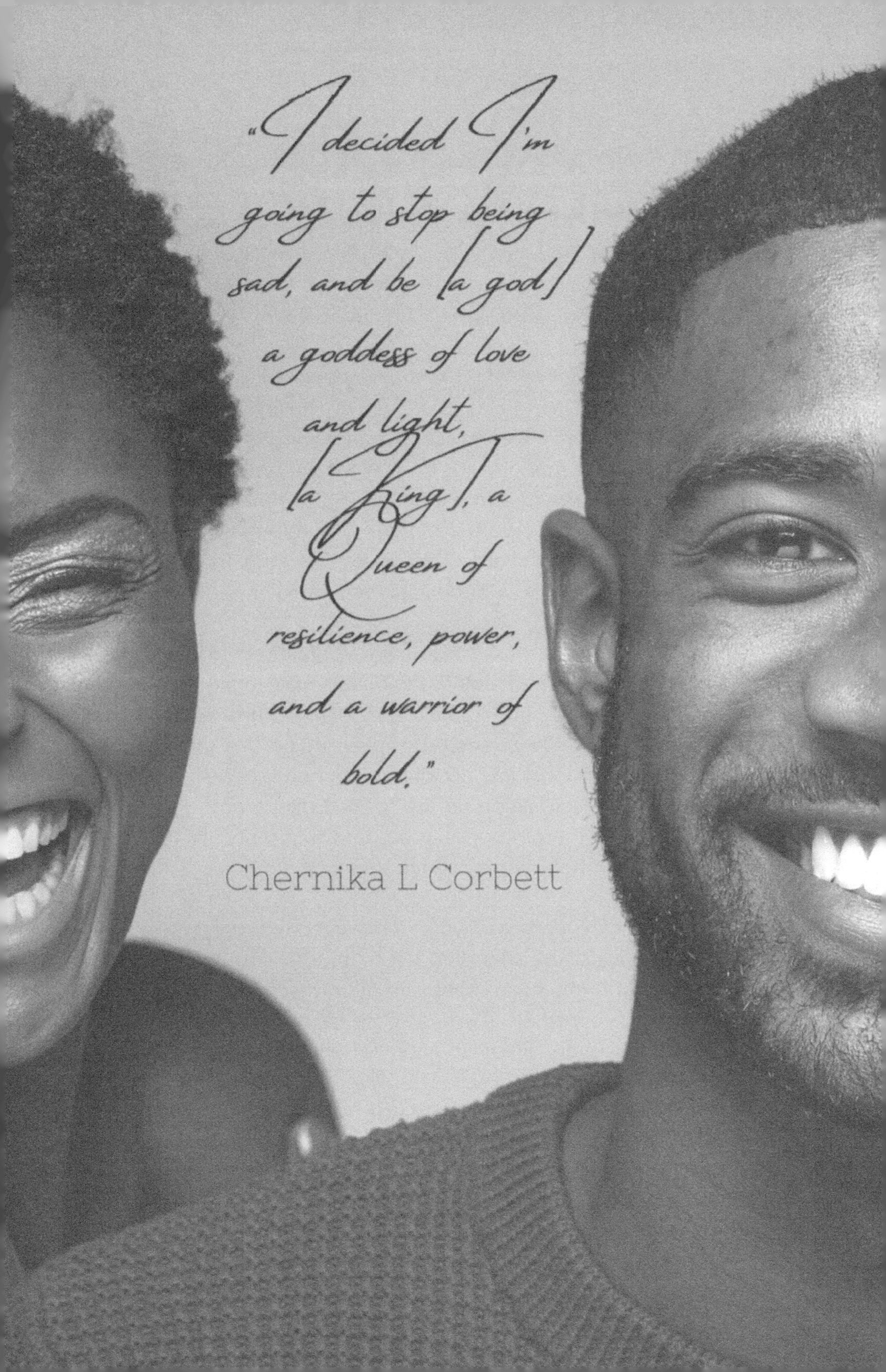
"I decided I'm
going to stop being
sad, and be [a god]
a goddess of love
and light,
[a King], a
Queen of
resilience, power,
and a warrior of
bold."
Chernika L Corbett

Get Rid of Negative Thoughts

Your mind is with you 24/7. Every millisecond. Every second. Every minute. Every hour of every day of every week, month, and year. An overwhelming amount of information is going in and out of your mind. You are *constantly*, *CONSTANTLY*, mulling over bits and pieces of information. We have the unique ability to relive and recreate experiences, twist scenarios, and create narratives in our heads that are not true. We have conversations that have not happened in expectation of a result that we may never encounter. We dream. We plan. We make inferences from actions and words. But where does this frame of mind get us? Tell me: how beneficial is overthinking?

On the opposite end, some think very little over the pieces of information that come their way and make feel-good, sometimes rash, and impulsive decisions (think about those purchases). Often, such people refuse to think about anything and commit to drowning out the noise in self-harming ways. Taking control of our minds and getting rid of negative thoughts should be our top priority. It's the most defining matter in every situation.

If you can conquer your negative thoughts, you will accomplish more than you ever dreamt. You must see the vision and maintain optimism towards its completion to conquer your goals. If you want to be debt-free, stress-free, and ignite your financial lifestyle, you have to think more positively about your ability to overcome your circumstances. Your mind is the most powerful asset you control. It gives you the ability to secure your dreams and shatter your goals.

Don't miss that. We have very little control over most things in life, but our minds are 100%, uniquely ours to think and manifest as we please. What thoughts will you yield to?

If you're fearful, your actions will be timid. If we want to be happy and see the beauty in our world, that's what we will do; appreciate the tiniest bloom in a run-down community. If you want to sulk, procrastinate, be a millionaire, become a doctor, then that's what you will do, followed by action. Your thoughts determine your outcomes.

For a few years, I was a complete mindset failure (listen to my radio interview at bonus.findyourspark.info), and when I look back, I see how I was trying to please everyone. And in doing so, I was failing, which made me feel defeated. I had a good word for everyone else, but for myself there were no rainbows or sunshine, just clouds and thunder storms. I felt overworked and underpaid. I was overworked —no one, not even the superiors, could deny this factor. Underpaid—well, I took a $20K pay cut and didn't have a meeting with myself that my lifestyle needed to change too. I was working 16- to 18-hour days, and the work was *still* incomplete. Tuh! I cringe thinking about it.

Journal Entry, 2015

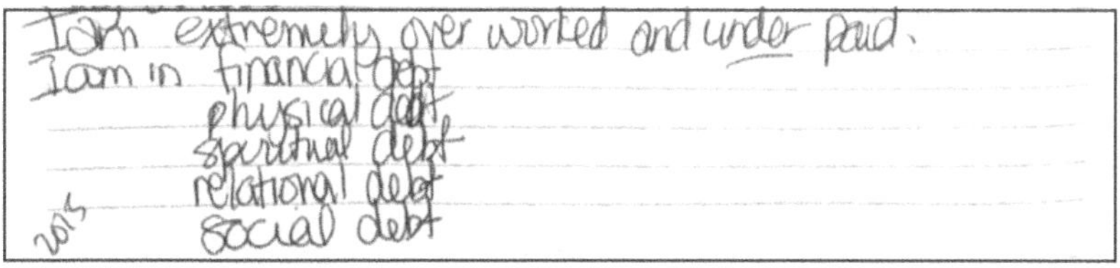
I am extremely over worked and under paid.
I am in financial debt
physical debt
spiritual debt
relational debt
2015 social debt

I was not thinking positively. I wasn't grateful for the many blessings I had. All I could see were problems, and that's *no bueño*.

My job was all I had, or so I thought. My livelihood was wrapped up in my performance as it had always been. My coworkers were even crying out to me! I tried to set boundaries, but the workload got worse. From there, I did not pull myself out of my miserable state of mind. I ran—not to deal with my issues but to numb. I focused on all the negative things happening around me and made some terrible life and financial choices that I would pay for years down the line. I made choices like traveling, partying, hanging with the wrong crowd (trust me; it costs!), inviting the wrong individ-uals into my personal space, making terrible dating choices, spending money on lavish objects, buying clothes, etc., all with future funds. I was in shambles, and my bank account showed it all!

But I smiled! And I looked good 'cause I was *killing* it at the gym, squats at 150lbs!

But inside, I was mi-ser-a-ble! It all looked good on the outside. People were like, "Ooh, she's coming out of her shell! I'm so proud of her!" Note: You will get many accolades when you look more like the crowd than when you stand alone. I was tired. An introvert trying to play an extrovert game will quickly time out. You can only wear a facade for so long. It wasn't until I made an effort to pick myself up that my life pivoted. I had to do all of the things we have discussed—everything. I had to have an awakening, and it wasn't pretty. But once I started thinking positively about where I wanted to go in life, that's when I started moving in a positive direction. It didn't come without consequences. It didn't come easy. Sulking was easy!

Eventually, I had the tough conversations. I removed myself from destructive environments, put up barriers, roadblocks, invited positive interactions, and cut ties to get to a better version of me. You see thinking positively and motivating yourself is time-consuming and intentional. You have to constantly block negative thoughts and see failures as opportunities, especially if you're trying to be the "*perfect people pleaser*." Don't expect to get it right every time, but expect that you'll get better every time you choose positive responses over negative ones.

Let's brainstorm. What will it take for you to drop the negative words and images you recycle and replace them with positive statements and experiences?

- Writing and saying daily affirmations are a place to start. You can use quotes or scriptures, write your goals, and post them where you can see them. (I have a sticky note wall.)
- Positive reinforcements. Find positive statements that you can say to yourself to deter negative thoughts quickly. When you think you're a failure or something terrible happens again, and you're thinking, "Why me? Why does this always happen to me?" That's a quick way to spiral down. You could say something like,
    - I'm okay. I'm going to be fine.
    - I can get out of this mess.
    - I can do this.
    - This is just a block in the road, but I'll get around it.
    - I know this happens, and not just to me.
    - Let me take a moment to figure this out.
    - I'm not going to let this get me down.
    - I'm not going to think this way.
    - I put myself here, and with help, I'll get through.
    - I am not okay at the moment, and that's okay.
    - Stop!"

  Yes, it takes all of this. It is a battle of the mind. You will have to repeat these sayings. If reading scripture helps (and it should try Psalms), then recite your favorite verse or read a chapter. If it's a mantra, then repeat that. Do what works. Repeat what you're saying over and over until it resonates. I have had to say, "I'm fine. It's okay many times.
- Keep your mind focused on the positives by focusing on what you can control vs. what you cannot. You have control over what you do, what you say, and how you think. Focus your efforts here. I don't care what someone did to you, even if they're wrong; focus on what you're going to do, say, and think.

My wall of goals and positive affirmations.

Difficult times will come, and you will grieve. However, if you practice and cultivate an optimistic lifestyle you will have an arsenal of routines to help you persevere. Wallowing for eternity is a recipe for living your worst life. You detract from yourself and others when you need to be attracting new energy, ideas, and hope for your future.

Once you take complete control over your mind and stop letting your circumstances and media control how you think and what you do, you'll be free of those negative thoughts and usher in positive energy—one of the most demanding shifts you can make as a human being.

Life is grim at times, and it's not always fair, either. Bad *-ish* happens to some of the sweetest spirits. The good people seem to get pushed back down over and over. Life is a symbiotic dance of bliss and blisters, and people will try to break you. However, your mind is the one area where it is essential to fight back. It's what keeps you in turmoil, but it's also what's going to get you out. Fill your entire being with encouraging messages of hope and strength, and strive to keep the cynical ones out, every day!

Write: What can you say to deter yourself from thinking negative thoughts? What actions can you take to think more positively? Search for positive quotes online or favorite verses and write them on sticky notes. Place them around your work desk, mirror, in your car, home office, near your bed, etc., where you will see and say them frequently.

Journal Entry, 2015

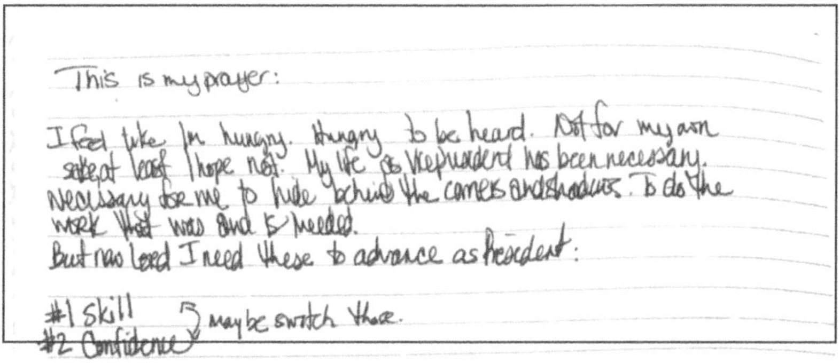
This is my prayer:

I feel like I'm hungry. Hungry to be heard. Not for my own sake at least I hope not. My life as Vice president has been necessary. Necessary for me to hide behind the corners and shadows. To do the work that was and is needed.
But now Lord I need these to advance as President:

#1 Skill
#2 Confidence } maybe switch those.

I had to come out of the dark shadows and start living life on different terms. So do you. When will you take the next step?

Ditch the *debtrimental* thoughts and embrace a life that enriches yourself, but more importantly others.

Find Your Voice: SAY NO!

Most of us have been taught to be pleasers growing up, especially in school. It's always the nonconforming kids who get in trouble (they also seem to breakout and do amazing things as adults). On the other hand, those who please the needs and wants of others are recognized and rewarded. Given the good 'ole pat on the back and the wink of the eye: good boy, good girl.

But sometimes this behavior can go overboard and actually be negative to our health and morale, along with other tenets of our lives. Did you know that being a people pleaser can actually be self-damaging? I've learned that pleasing can be a form of perfectionism. And though it may seem like a noble battle to be perfect, it's actually quite self-destructing and quite opposite of its name because the focus is never about you; it's always about the other person.

Perfection is often the enemy of greatness.
Janelle Monáe

I run across many lines in my journals that solidify that trying to be perfect is crippling. You become focused on being and doing right, according to other people's philosophies. All the while, you subjugate yourself to the opinions of others and then form those ideals as your thoughts of self (self-worth and efficacy). How miserable and self-demeaning is that? We all need to love ourselves in a way that makes others catch their breath–the audacity!

There is a constant battle to be perfect, correct, and worthy of everyone around you. There's nothing wrong with wanting to help and do great work for others, but we have to make sure that it's for the right reasons. We have to be careful of putting our needs and beliefs aside to adopt others. There is an imbalance when we fail to take good care of our emotional needs and self-care in general. Why should anyone respect you if you won't respect yourself?

We have to stop saying *yes* to everyone else's dreams, aspirations, and good times and say NO to accomplish our dreams and goals.

In writing, this may seem like such an easy task, but true *pleasers* will find themselves self-sabotaging their success by going back to save and help others. Stop! There's a time for that, but first, finish your journey, complete your goals, and get your healing!

On the journey to taking control of your financial lifestyle, you must block paths that led you there. Saying *no* to people is one step. But you have to say *no* to some lousy habits that got you there in the first place (for me overspending, lack of planning, no savings, using credit cards hazardously, and racking up debt).

I challenge you to set some boundaries and make your word ***NO*** for the next several months of the year. Watch how your life changes. Document it. Great things will happen, and even some unseeingly bad things may be for your good.

Note: You're not saying *no* for the sake of saying *no*. You're saying *no* to things that rob your time, misalign with your goals, and cross the lines you've set for your life. It's all about setting healthy boundaries.

When you start saying *no*, it's going to upset some people in your life. I say, "the quickest way to see who's for you is to tell them about your dreams and begin speaking up for yourself!" Sit back and watch.

People are addicted to the benefits you provide from having a lack of boundaries.

Some will see it as a personal attack—beware. In the same breath, those who care for you will congratulate and encourage you to continue. In completing this one gesture, you will find strength and begin to exert more control over your life. Speaking up and setting boundaries will look good on you. That's the new sexy! That's my new love language! I want you to put it on like your favorite outfit and rock it.

I'm not telling you this without experience. I made my word *no* for a year (2019). Specifically, I aimed to control my finances by not traveling, no matter how desirable, unless it was a drive away: no airplanes, no big trips. I decided I wasn't going to eat out as much or go to events I was accus-tomed to, like theatrical plays, going out with friends to shows, or accepting tons of invites to parties. I was focused on my baking (finding my peace, plotting, and planning) and spending as little as possible. Plus, I wanted to start putting money aside in my savings account. I even decided to stop spending so much money on other people and gifting only to children. I had to get my whole house (financially and spiritually) in order. Buying extravagant gifts and trying to please people, buying drinks for everyone, paying other's bills, alongside paying one-hundred-dollar interest rates, was not cute (at all), definitely not *boss*!

Too many of us are out here trying to flaunt, floss, and front for others on our jobs, in our circles, for our family, associat-es, and people we don't even know or like (Tell the truth!)! It ain't cute! We are too grown out here to be running around caring about how people see us who have no real invest-ment or value in our livelihood.

Zero.

At some point, you have to get serious and ask yourself, what are you doing? Or one of my favorite memes, "*What is you doing baby, noo*!"

Sir, Ma'am, stop!

Instead of focusing on others, decide what kind of life you want to live. Paycheck to paycheck or debt-free? Debt-free and just paying the bills, or debt-free with a healthy savings account? Debt-free with no emergency fund or debt-free living off dividends? Or are you okay with simply making ends meet? Are you willing to continue to trade your time for money while others have the freedom of time because their money makes money?

You decide: Which stress are you willing to manage?

It's pretty stressful (in a good way) to think you can be debt-free—the audacity to dream of being a millionaire (billionaire, let's step it up). It's stressful to think differently about what you want for your life, especially when it is so different from what's around you and how people are used to seeing you. Before finishing this book, I met a gentleman on social media who proved my theory correct. He runs a program trying to help people change their low-income status. He was helping someone with the idea of being more self-sufficient, and their significant other came down to his office to have "*some words" b*ecause of the beliefs he was pumping into their partner's mind! Thank goodness nothing transpired, but you see my point. Ideas are scary!

Belief systems are what get great leaders trying to promote positive change assassinated.

It's time for us to grow. It's time for you to succeed. You're not that little child anymore, being seen and not heard. Think about your great-ness. Adopt it as your belief system. Now, speak up, and use the voice God gave you to take control over your life. I repeat:

Speak up, and use the voice God gave you to take control over your life.

#Boundaries ◆#BoundariesSquad ◆ #AmplifyYourVoice ◆#StraightenYourCrown

Was that loud enough?

We take control by saying *no* to ourselves as well as others. You need to say *no* to practices that kill your time, steal your energy, and keep you in turmoil. If you have negativity around you, say *no* to that crowd and find some positive energy. You can't live up to your full potential with words that destroy your spirit.

What's causing you stress? How can you relieve some of that by saying no? I had to quit my job and move to a less stressful environment. I had to say no from being overworked, under-acknowledged, and not fully appreciated, breaking the cardinal rule of finding a job first —I had to get out and rest my faith in the Almighty. And when I did, I landed my dream job that I wrote down maybe two or three years earlier! I told y'all: Put the pen to the paper!

When you start saying *no*, you take back a little power for yourself.

> **Side note:** Don't feel like you have to explain your *no,* either. It's just *no*. Plain and simple.

I admit, you will feel guilty at first (especially if you're a pleaser and not accustomed to being assertive), but in due time, you'll be okay saying it. Hopefully, one day you'll be okay hearing it from others, too. The way you're going to ditch stress and ditch debt to live a richer lifestyle is by beginning to say *no* to the unhealthy mindsets and practices that got you into your current circumstances.

I say this often, "*The world will teach you how to get into debt. Your family and friends will encourage your debt. And the creditors will profit from your debt until you have the courage to say NO.*"

Pick up your crown and exert that *no* like a boss. It's not about being arrogant, it's about protecting what's precious. It's about taking care of you. You were formed from His own image for His glory. Fix that crown and don't let two letters keep you from your greatness!

Warning: Setting boundaries has its benefits, but it also has a downside. You may lose out. You may lose contacts, benefits, business, partnerships, friends, family members, etc. You might lose out on some experiences and spending time with others. This step is not easy or pretty. You might be accused of being mean, or wrong, and called all sorts of names for the sake of self-care. But I encourage you to stay the course.

Greatness lies in being uncomfortable. **Recap**: fire welds metal into beautiful sculptures. Some things must be put in the fire so their true beauty can be revealed.

Continue down the path you started, and don't forget to invite quality friends or even a professional into your life if the fire gets too hot.

Write: Make a plan. In what areas do you need to say *no*? Where and with whom do you need to set boundaries? What will this look like? What are the consequences of saying *no*?

Go ahead, let's hear you say it: NO! And put some respect on it when you do!

Get Organized

People may laugh if they see my organizational structure. My friends know it's really organized chaos. I have a system, dagnabbit! The chaos of receipts during tax time is unraveling, structuring a business properly can feel like climbing Mount Everest, handling paying your bills before the lights get turned off is flat-out *stress*-ful (especially when money is tight), and balancing your schedule among house chores can be downright discombobulating! How do we do it all? We haven't mentioned jumbling other's lives (kids, significant others, dating, friends, aging parents, etc.) in the midst of our own. And don't even think about including being a good citizen and trying to keep up with politics, which life matters, who to vote for, and supporting every hashtag human rights campaign. Breathe! It's downright disrespectful with all the stuff we must complete. Geez! How do we keep it all together?

Get organized. Better said than done! I get it! Organization is another critical aspect of reducing stress.

Believe it or not, humans love structure. You're more successful when you're organized and everything is displayed invitingly. You find items easier in retail stores, making shopping more enjoyable. It's less of a headache when you can have all of your tax documents to file your return. When you can glance down at a schedule or list and checkoff items from it, there's a feeling of satisfaction! Even the energy in your house will flow better when you're in an organized and clean environment.

We cannot control everything in our lives, but we can establish some strategic methods to calm the chaos. Here are a few tips to start you on your organizational journey:

Make Your Bed: This straightforward yet redundant act sets the tone in your most private space. Don't beat yourself up if you're rushing and forget to do so (this is my struggle area; when I do it, I feel accomplished!). The simple act of making your bed is relaxing. Now, you will need to get out of bed to do this, so roll over and get your day started! It will change the whole outlook of your bedroom. You'll feel lighter. Sing a tune, say some affirmations, listen to your spiritual songs or favorite podcasts while you do it. The goal here is to clear your space of negative energy. Making your bed is a form of cleaning up; that's all. It includes cleaning the funk off the dresser, floor, closets, etc., to clearing the atmosphere—preparing it for productivity. Personally, it allows my mind to think clearly without the negative energy from clutter. I fall off the wagon in this area a lot (lol), but it feels *so* good when I do it (#noshame). The goal, however, is to add some positive energy to your space! Don't forget to let in some bright light; even a glimmer brings hope and enlightens your mood!

Lists, lists, and more lists! Lists are tricky. They help, but they can be overwhelming, too. Here's the deal: make a list and then decide on the top items you must complete that day. Don't go down to the easy projects (#guilty); do the most critical tasks on the list first. Everything else is second nature. If you follow this advice, you will be in the winner's circle. But if you're a graduate of the University of Procrastination like me (I have a Ph.D. from U of P.), you might be tempted to dance around your list and then begin to make new lists, getting it all done except for the top items. The prime duties are probably your most daunting tasks, so schedule them on separate days if possible.

I make a list of bills (see below) I need to pay monthly (divided up by the beginning and end of the month, or when I'm paid), so I don't have to think about it. I click the bubble next to the listed item and digitally check it off`on my phone as I pay each. When I leave it up to my memory, that's when I forget to pay a bill, and whelp, trouble begins.

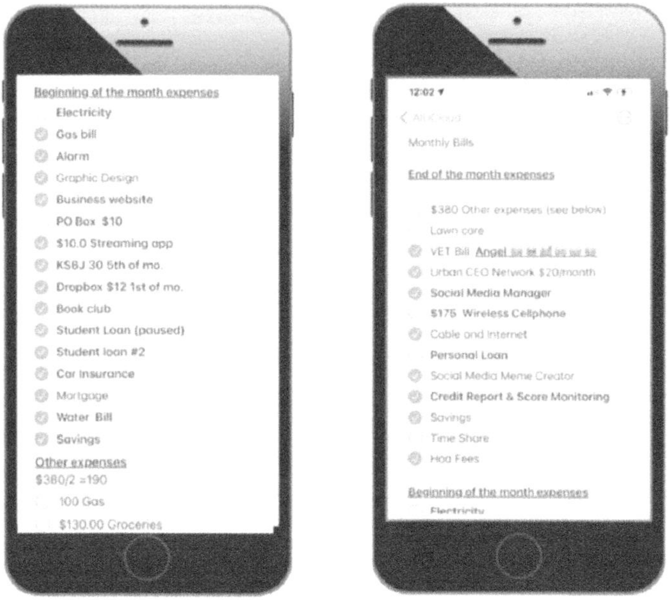

Schedule Your Life: I use a digital calendar to schedule whatever I'm doing. Some people love to get a tangible planner and jazz it up with stickers and notes (almost like a diary). Go with what works. I have tried both, but I don't carry my planner with me everywhere. So, the best planner for me is on my phone because it's usually near me. I am more successful when I schedule parts of my life. Notice I said *parts* because scheduling some things would add more stress to my life. I might have "clean up" on the list, but planning that at a specific time would cause me to skip over it; however, it may feel blissful for you—schedule tasks as strictly or as loosely as needed.

Designate a place for things: Get rid of that junk drawer now! The junk drawer in the kitchen drives me nuts, so I made sure I don't have one. When items do not have a place, they just get thrown everywhere. This is an area of improvement for me at home because I have so many things, like pins, pens, gifts from work, etc. I found three single-hole punchers in different "organized boxes" one day and thought to myself, why? "Because you're an educator," that little voice said! Finding a spot for sticky notes, pens, tape, shoes, clothes, and more will keep the junk pile from growing. Have you looked at the products you have under the bathroom sink? It can get crowded and dysfunctional quickly when things don't have an area. Destressing is the goal. And cleaning is a task that gives us more control over our environment. We may not like to do it, but the energy is different when every-thing has a place. You like finding items without ripping up your house, right? We claim small wins when we organize. You will not believe how relieving it feels to accomplish small tasks like decluttering.

Clean out the clutter: I recently have decided to move toward a more minimalist lifestyle (it hasn't taken full effect yet) and thus cleaned out my closet resorting in about seven thirty-two-gallon bags of apparel and shoes. Whew! The weight lifted off of me felt good. Why do we accumulate so many things? Clutter is chaos. Chaos disrupts your flow of thinking clearly, leading to a continuous state of anxiety and built-up pressure. We may think this has nothing to do with money habits, but it does. You have to decrease stress and bring more endorphins to your life so you can think clearly and get a handle on your finances. It will also be a great lesson concerning the money you spend on useless items.

How many gadgets do you own that you don't use? Or how many clothes do you have with the tags still on them? Use them or get rid of them—sell them on an app or social media. Hoarding, as we have seen from the television series, is about your mindset. Decluttering will relax you and put you at ease, but if it's causing you stress, seek professional help because hoarding is real.

Clean up: I can't tell you how perfect life feels when you have no dishes in the sink, those diamond lines etched out in the carpet, laundry done, bathrooms on point, no dusty tabletops, and so on. It feels like gold! No matter how ginormous or bite-size your space is, you cannot deny that a clean house feels fantastic!

To take control of your life, finances, and stress levels, set aside the time needed to get organized and clean. You may need to hire someone or solicit help from friends if you're overwhelmed. When you exert control over your life, you usher in self-care. And who can take care of your internal being better than you?

Write: In what area of your life do you need to organize? What can you do to get organized today?

Tell the Money Where to Go

We can't control everything in our lives, but we can take the reins in many areas. There are right-hand problems that are well within our reach. After exerting control over your mind, your voice, and your schedule of tasks, it's now time to take control over your money and build a better financial lifestyle. And it is a lifestyle. We're still trying to straighten our crowns now!

You can live in financial chaos or exert financial control. Which do you want? Which do you deserve? It's time to tell our money where to go to control our stress and finances.

Other entities will take your money if you fail to make a game plan. The government has a plan for your money. The car salesman has a plan for your money. Your son/daughter's school has a plan for your money (remember those fundraisers, school events, pictures, class parties, projects, field trips, etc.). Did you tell the IRS how much of your taxes to take out of your check? They, too, have a plan for your money. Do you have to tell the bank the fees to extract when you go over the limit? Does inflation wait for you to get a raise before it raises prices? Or, do your friends make sure you can afford to go out before they ask you to the upscale all-white party?

Everyone has a plan for your money.

When was the last time you refused to buy into the big business schemes of society that preys on your money at least once a month? Don't believe me? January, you shop the White Sale. In February, you shop for Valentines' Day. In March, you celebrate March Madness or buy extra beer for St. Patrick's Day. Oh, did we forget to put out the eggs for Easter this year? Mother's Day and Father's Day close us out before we end school for the summer. July, let's pull out our grills, have a cookout, and buy fireworks. And it's summer, so we have to take a vacation, right? We'll talk more about this in Chapter 7, but you get the point!

Overall, who checks with you before asking you to spend your money? Hopefully, you. But so many of us don't. We allow life to happen to us instead of taking the time to plan where our money should go strategically. Try skipping a few holidays or celebrations. Can you do it? You're probably feeling guilty just thinking about it and even convincing yourself that giving is your love language to justify spending extravagantly.

If the giving is causing you to be broke,
you better control that love language.

You should not have to overly spend money to show you love someone, especially if that's what's keeping you in debt. How much money could you save if you avoid spending in these areas? I dare you to go back through your bank state-ments and calculate how much you waste each year on items like gifts, parties, events, eating out, decorations, clothes, work-related items, and so on. You probably had enough money to ditch the debt in some key areas, so you could secure your future, have more for healthcare, and save for your child's future or a future project. Whether you're single or married, you need to control the money you earn. Picture how much better your gifts will be when you don't have any debt. When you're not operating in a life full of stress, how much easier could you help your family or friends without it feeling like three steps backward?

STOP: Look at your bank and credit card statements for the last three months. Where could you have saved some money? What do you need to cut out? Where can you take control? Once you decide to make some changes, where will you put the money you're saving?

Again, talk to your money, and tell him where he has to go. Yes, that's right: let Ben know that you're commanding the ship now and that there are some household rules he must follow! Let no one decide where your money goes except for you: not your friends, big business, the church (I didn't say God), the school, any salesman, etc., but you (I mean, you still have to pay taxes, but there are some advantages out there; keep reading).

Money is a tool, as are all other resources here on earth. Controlling how you spend should be rational, diplomatic, and void of emotion—for the most part, because you'll be full of emotions when you pay off your last debt! When you make decisive choices that put you in a better position financially, how much easier is it to give cheerfully (2 Corinthians 9:7)? If you only spend emotionally, you'll find that you spend more of your time laboring over expenses you could not afford, and you will spend more of your time in a stress-related environment and state of mind.

As I mentioned earlier, know what triggers you to emotionally spend, and be aware of this trap that many (rich and poor) succumb to every day. Emotional decisions are often ones of regret, and they usually provide very little return on your money (by experience and levels of joy). Many of these emotional expenditures give us split-second highs when we purchase them and a few moments of awe from those who admire us. When we spend emotionally, it's usually a liability instead of an asset. But for the rich and mighty, even those glamorous assets bought in a rush can be a devastating financial decision.

Strategy trumps emotional spending.

Sometimes we can simplify our lives by just asking:

Is it a need or a want?

Do I have to have it now or later?

If I don't get it, what will happen?

So how do we take control and tell our money where to go? Easy! Okay, maybe not so easy because it takes time to develop a new mindset and take action. Some ways to take control:

- **Build an emergency fund.** Call it whatever you want like *Pandora's box.* Life happens, so prepare like Joseph. **Keep up with your cash flow.** Know what comes in and what comes out of your accounts.
- **Budget**. No one likes to hear this word, but the only budget that works is the one that works! Give yourself an allowance in every area, from groceries to your shoe fetish.
- **Begin investing**. Begin researching where to put your investments. Allocate monthly funds into your investment accounts.
- **Balance your spending.** When you buy something, make sure it's for you. Are you purely flossin', stuntin', and fakin' for others, or do you genuinely enjoy the gift? How will you know? Well, if no one ever saw what you purchased, and you didn't get any *oohs*, *aahs*, fire emojis, or "That's *dope" comments*, etc., about it, would you still be okay? Seeking attention from others is an emotional trait that can cause you to spend irrationally, keeping you out of balance.
- **Know what's on your credit report.** Then work to clean it up if you plan to use it to lower your interest rates or buy additional assets--money making assets.
- **Aggregate your debts.** And then tackle them one by one.
- **Set goals.** Your money goals will fuel the decisions you make.
- **Speak with a financial expert** based on your needs.

need a plan for your estate after your passing? Are you focused on retirement? Are you in a place to invest? Do you have enough insurance in case something happens to you? Maybe you want to get out of debt, but you don't know where to start. Financial help is unlimited when you start searching and asking for assistance.

There are different types of experts. You may need a financial coach like myself if you're trying to get out of debt and budget. A financial advisor can help build your wealth and make sure you invest in a way to help you retire. Estate planners can help you secure your hard-earned money if something fatal should happen to you and when you pass on. Money gurus exist in every area: insurances, auto, taxes, mortgages, bankruptcy, debt, credit, bookkeeping, stocks, bonds, student loans, foreign taxes, etc. so, don't be afraid to seek help with money issues—most of us weren't taught these things in school.

Just make sure you ask the right questions and that the person you work with is acting on your behalf. People who are fiduciary advisors and agents have pledged to act on behalf of their clients. Advisors have strict rules set up by FINRA (Financial Industry Regulatory Authority), but it's still your duty to vet those working with your money. I know many times as educators wealth advisors show up at our jobs on lunch breaks. Just because they're at your place of employment does not mean their right for you. Ask if your agent is a fiduciary looking out for your best interest. Like you get to know your partner, come with questions for people and institutions working with you and your money goals.

Are the products they're recommending for your benefit or theirs? How will they be paid? What fees should you expect? Do some research and check what's appropriate to ask, depending on the expert you need.

As a financial coach, I continuously align myself with other experts to point future clients in the right direction. Such coaches teach basic financial literacy and behavioral aspects of finances such as budgeting, ditching debt, accountability, bankruptcy, purchasing a home, saving, dealing with collection agencies, setting boundaries with money), role playing tough money conversations, and more depending on their expertise.

Remember: When we take care of our minds and habits, we arm ourselves with ammunition to care for our financial health and overall well-being. Taking control is not about perfection; it's about giving you a proactive way to deal with the hardships which arise. Talk to the money, tell it where to go, and the money will work for you.

Write: Which area do you need to work on the most right now? Negative thoughts, saying no, getting organized, or telling your money where to go? What steps are you prepared to take?

CHAPTER VI:

Time: Your Richest Asset

There aren't a lot of equalizers in this world, but time is one of them. We all have the same amount of time. However, how we choose to fill this precious commodity that we have is what makes the difference. It separates the *haves* from the *have nots*. You've heard it over and over. It's your richest asset. If you spend all your time brewing over negative thoughts, what do you expect to become of it? If you spend time decreasing your stress, what will happen? If you spend time working on your financial goals, what will become of them? If you spend time building your online store, listening to uplifting podcasts, reading *Find Your Spark: 7 Steps to Ditch Stress and Ignite Your Financial Lifestyle,* working on positive relationships, reading enriching content on how to think and live a better financial life, what will become of all of that time you spent? (Did you catch the allusion? Lol!)

How you spend your time is the number one qualifier in your life. I don't care where you were born or what you have access to at this moment. The utilization of your time will define who you want to be, where you want to go, and how you're going to get there. Evaluate what you did with your time in the past thirty days—that's what your future looks like if you don't make some changes. We have to start committing more to ourselves, plan out our time on paper or utilizing apps, prioritizing what needs to get done and get P.A.I.D. (read on). Enough with the excuses: execute and excel!

"Change will not come if
we wait for some other person
or some other time. We are
the ones we've been waiting
for. We are the change that
we seek."
Barack Obama

Overcommitting

Have you ever wanted to save the world (especially after watching documentaries), help your neighbor, be head of the parent committee, build a business, fight crime, write a book, take a class, write a grant, be a good auntie, or uncle, lobby to congress, be a great friend and sibling, support your significant other, get that degree, save the zoo animals, protect the wildlife, and learn a new skill at the same time? Do you say *yes* to everyone? Does it drive you crazy? If you're anything like me, you find yourself overcommitting to too many tasks:

- Achievements you want to undertake.
- Commitments you feel obligated to say *yes* to.
- Some deeds you complete out of fear, peer pressure, or regret.

When we overcommit ourselves, we pile an astronomical amount of stress on our shoulders. Being the go-to person can be stressful, handling everyone's problems, including your own. We have a super-hero syndrome when we repeatedly help everyone else. After a while—and this could be years—we tend to fall under burdensome pressure. For a time, you may be able to maintain, might even thrive at hitting each goal, and then life happens: emergencies arise, and our world begins unraveling, or we get burned out and remain stagnant, dropping the ball in multiple areas of our lives. And even during this time, people will still *ask their asks*. Unbelievable!

Ultimately, when we overcommit, defeated mindsets can sink in, even shame. We deplete ourselves of financial, spiritual, physical, and mental resources.

Often throughout all the chaos, we refuse to stop and remind ourselves that we are one person; we can always say *no*, delegate work, and invite others to assist us along the way.

Depending on your personality, you may choose to do all, some, or none of these choices. However, we must realize that it's not in our best interest to be overworked and overcommitted.

When you find yourself in such dilemmas, try to ask yourself what jobs are least important or what you could relinquish. Which assignments can you delegate to someone else or back to the original owner? Try to rank what's most important to least significant, according to you. Look at your timeline for completion of each responsibility, which is due now vs. later? Also, consider the impact that each task carries. We can free ourselves from stressful situations, but we must learn not to get into them in the first place. Know how much you can handle. If it feels like too much before you commit, then it probably is best to refuse. You have the power to keep yourself from overcommitting by saying *no*. Go ahead; try it!

Write: I often overcommit myself in these areas:

____

____

____

My goal is to release myself from the following task of

____

by: (Include the actions and time frame it will take.)

____

____

____

Streamline Your Time

You're already aware that putting your life on a calendar and making lists will help you get organized and reduce the anxiety running through your mind. Some people might even say that a calendar would cause them added stress. Generally speaking, this may be a valid response for people who are not used to adhering to schedules, time, rules, or bound to others (#guilty). Organized people are more productive. I've watched an organized mother of four get more done by noon than most people get done their entire day! No matter if you're a free spirit or a rule follower, if you get it down on the calendar and streamline your time, you will find that your workload will improve. Besides, that's part of life, right, getting stuff. done?

There are so many apps on the market that will help you to be more time-efficient. Find one (maybe two) and stick with them! I use the calendar on my phone to record alerts and schedule essential items. If it is not on my calendar, yikes!

Financially speaking, some items to put on your calendar could be a reminder of when you need to:

- pay a company or yourself,
- step by step what you need to get done that day (by time),
- calls you need to make,
- follow-ups,
- appointments,
- automatic debits,
- donations,
- school fundraisers,
- when you need cash,

- daily mantras,
- positive messages,
- or my favorite—when I need to cancel a free subscription (lol, don't play)!

Other items include your family's schedule, training, quiet time, exercise, free time, dates, doctor appointments, and so on. Being able to see all that you have to do keeps you from continuously having to hold so much information in your short-term memory, which can cause you to forget and add stress. You can also look back to see how much you have accomplished. Below you can see some of the tasks from my actual calendar, like who to pay, a positive affirmation, and some other educational meetings. Having this at my fingertips increases my productivity! Try it!

Make sure you not only schedule the calendar but add an alert. Alerts are gentle reminders to complete our work. I give myself at least two alerts (I can get easily distracted). If you have a habit of hitting snooze or ignoring your alerts, stop! Take time out to look at them and do the task. If you need to, add a reminder to do the job later, so you don't forget. We live busy lives, and it's easy to keep plunging straight ahead.

Breathe.

The goal here is by scheduling and reminding yourself with alerts and making lists to do your necessary duties. You will save time and money and decrease your stress. If you are not so keen on apps or calendars and can afford to hire someone to help you get your life straight, like an assistant or life coach, do that. There are people with superpowers who will help you stay organized and teach you how to be organized according to your personality to manage your time more effectively. Do the work, and you'll find that you have less time to stress and more time to enjoy life.

Prioritize and Reprioritize

I know by now you made a list, right? I hope so! Now that there are hundreds of overwhelming tasks in front of us, who needs a break? Making a list is like going off into a fantasy world. When is it going to get done? What will get done first? And who's going to do it all? You, of course! After you get it down, immediately prioritize which jobs get completed now vs. later.

Prioritizing life is a very long journey. Many factors will determine which items from your list get priority. But prioritizing is a must! If you refuse to prioritize, the easiest and less important things get done first, while the more laborious and mind-boggling jobs will accumulate. By now, you know what happens when work amasses (like taxes, ugh). Let's chop that fantasy list down into smaller portions and focus on what needs to be done today. Make sure it is absolutely a top priority to put on your daily list. Narrow your list to your top three or five tasks and rank those in order from most important to least important. You can do this every day for different`areas of your life and even have categories (e.g., work, home, social, etc.) to help you prioritize, which is important.

In the same fashion, use this method to classify your finances. Determine which bills and debts are due now, what can wait, and so forth if you are in a tight squeeze. Hopefully, that tight squeeze will be eliminated by careful financial planning, prioritizing, and building an emergency fund. These are hidden jewels when it comes to managing your time effectively.

Get P.A.I.D.

You know the cliche: Time is money. If you get more time, in essence, the more money you could make. The more time you waste, the less time you have. So, I ask, which is more significant time or money? I'll let you decide on that. But if we look at society, it seems that those who have more time (to do what they truly want) are often well off—having`time for ministry, leisure, family, and business.

Essentially, if *they* can keep you busy, *they* will keep you depleted, robbing you of creativity and your dreams. *Who are they*? Anything or anyone that distracts you from finding your spark and living your very best life. The more time you spend working at other people's jobs, working on other people's dreams and problems, fixating on other's drama, etc., the further you are from where you truly want to be in life. We have to find ways to get our time back. So that we too can relish in peace and mindfulness. Let's get P.A.I.D. by streamlining the way we utilize our most precious commodity: time.

Plan: There is no magic here. If you want to be successful in any way possible, you must plan your course. It's like targeting your route to your dreams. Paying off`debt needs a plan. Being stress-free needs a plan. Building a business needs a plan. Having a better relationship needs a plan. Got it! Can you *will* yourself to be debt-free? Can you wake up and say, "*okay, no more stress*," and then poof, gone! And I imagine building a business or a wonderful relationship doesn't happen just because we want it to either. We have to work at anything we want in this life.

Write down the plan like it's a playbook, and run the play.

For me to be stress-free and embark on a debt-free journey, I had to focus by planning and targeting both of these areas. I had to talk, use my voice, take control, and manage my finances and time (a mountainous struggle). Your plan may start sloppy with just words or a few sentences. However, if you can get it down on paper, you can make it work. Write it down no matter how it comes out. **Think**: What do you need to do to win in this domain? If there's an area of uncertainty: research it, ask questions, hire an expert, talk to quality people, or find a group of like-minded people. Write it down like a recipe, or bulleted list, or steps. Brainstorm with a positive and forward-thinking friend if necessary. And as you continue on your journey, refine your plans to match your goals. Remember, you can't run any play if you don't have any plays in your playbook! An Olympian doesn't win the day of the competition. Olympians win on game day four years prior by executing their day-to-day plans. On game day, the culmination of their training is in motion. Imagine the motivation it takes to focus for such an extended amount of time. What planned sacrifices and challenges will you accomplish?

Affirmation: I'm committed to making plans for my future. I'm committed to running the play.

Allow Flexibility: Once we have a plan, we want it to come together how we planned it and, in more haste than we dreamt it. Slow down, playa! Slow—it—down. Anytime you make a plan, know there are going to be minute and major setbacks. Be flexible. It is okay to bend a little from what you intended. In the quest to quell your financial indebtedness, your credit score may go down, a forgotten debt may pop up, you may have to slow down on your investments, or even reach for that emergency fund. You might need to incorporate ideas from experts to increase your financial knowledge. Maybe your idea has flaws, won't work, or needs altering. It's okay. You're going to be fine. Just know that things will work out if you keep to your intended agenda and allow some flexibility.

Sometimes, we will even have to go back to step one because of roadblocks. At this point, we have to decide if we are still willing and capable of redeveloping our plan and continuing the course. Overall, don't lose sight of your objective. Let your ambition, wise council, and adaptability propel you toward your goals. Besides, we do not want to lose time focusing on matters, which sideswipes us from our mission. Have a willingness to compromise to keep your ambitions moving forward.

Ignore Distractions: It has been a journey writing this text during quarantine. The distractions were vast, stemming from all areas of life: procrastination, family, friends, deaths, health, human rights protests, viruses, money issues, social media, disputes, and opportunities; the list is endless. What was supposed to take a short amount of time took me well over a year to accomplish because I allowed distractions to consume me. It wasn't until I ignored distractions, with some God interventions, informal coaching, and focusing on my plan did I accomplish my vision. That meant I couldn't buy everything I wanted, take trips even though I had the funds, eat out at every whim, or even hang out with friends at every request. My focus to finish meant I missed out on what everyone else was doing.

If you can't ignore distractions, you will be consumed and fail. Set up your horse blinders and stick to the plans you set out to conquer.

One of the biggest distractions we have is access to the internet. We invite so much into our homes and lives by being plugged into our electronic devices. Some of us work online, and it's our way of life. However, you don't have to let it distract you. Make a plan when you get online. What do you need to do? Write it down if necessary. Sometimes, when I'm switching apps or tabs, I have to remind myself what I'm supposed to be doing, or I could quickly lose an hour.

Do you have friends or family members who are a distraction to your goals? If so, find time and space to be alone to do your work. Be honest and upfront with them, letting them know you need time to yourself. You may have to turn down opportunities so that you can meet your deadlines and goals. Therefore, you cannot say yes to everything. You must have self-control; you must exert boundaries.

I love the image displayed in Proverbs 25:28 (KJV), which says, "*He that hath no rule over his own spirit is like a city that is broken down, and without walls.*" You cannot allow anything to come into your heart, your home, your eyes, your mind. It is the thin line between success and failure. Giving your attention away to distractions will rob you of your precious time and money. Time is given to each of us every day we awake from our rest. How will you manage it?

Please note: You still need to take time out to be with others and build relationships. Finding the balance to do so is how you make sure you eliminate distractions. When it's time to work, work, and when it's time to play, play.

Decompress: Can you imagine the deep and darkened anxiety and angst it took to run away as a slave, to exist as a slave? They were always on guard because, at any moment, their life could be taken. Rest: When did they *really* get to rest? Being watched and controlled keeps you on alert. My ancestors had to make do under harsh circumstances. But now, we say we're *free* and still find ourselves in relationships and systems that model control and domination over every aspect of our lives. See, being in a state of anxiety for long periods is detrimental to your physical health, mental health, and spiritual being. Remember, if *they* can keep you busy, it's easier to shut down your dreams. It's easier to forget your purpose or never find it in the first place. Envision the poem "Dream Deferred" by Langston Hughes as he talks about dreams:

"Does it dry up like a raisin in the sun?
Or fester like a sore—...?"

If you are filled with anxiety, how can you hold onto your dreams? How do you have time to plan? When does life become enjoyable? You are a different person under stress than when you are at ease and comfortable. You see the world differently. You think about life differently. You hear nature, sounds, and discussions differently. You even dream differently. (Thank God my ancestors got to a *version* of freedom so that they too could dream and decompress. So that I could dream and partake in the *pursuit of happiness* and *economic liberty*!)

You have to allow moments of decompression so that you can have balance in your life. This process is different for everyone. Some may enjoy a trip or playing games, eating out, reading, interacting on social media, exercising, sitting in silence, taking a nap, driving without aim, reading scripture, thinking (with no stimuli), getting beauty treatments, or simply talking with family or friends. If you never take time to relax, moments of epiphany will come to you the least. It is in the times of nothingness and simplicity that you engineer significant ideas. The pandemic provided the perfect atmosphere for such moments to occur, which is how so many people found time to alter their lives for the better. How did you use that time? Did you cultivate some of it to decompress? Find time to find peace, be calm, reduce the pressure in your life, so you can reclaim the time you need to conquer greatness.

Write: What is your greatest hindrance to managing your time? What steps do you need to take to fix this problem?

PAUSE HERE

Before you go any further, I implore you to take a moment and listen to this segment of the book.

Yes, stop! Go to your bonus materials at bonus.findyourspark.info and listen to the *Believe in Yourself* **Podcast**. Also, download the free version or order a copy of the *Master Your Money* workbook.

Take great notes for this next section.

Are you refreshed?

Let's go!

CHAPTER VII:

Mastering your Finances: Make, Manage, and Maximize Your Money!

I can pretty much bank on the fact that everyone knows how to make money. We all know how to get to the bag, as we say when it comes to getting a job! The education system teaches us how to get the dollar by working for someone else. Somehow, we miss the ball when using the talents we already have inside us to create cash. Furthermore, far too many people fail to have any restraint or proper education about keeping their money. And too many of us lack the knowledge on exponentially growing our money.

If you want to ditch your stress and live a healthier financial lifestyle, you need to take action on these three aspects: earn, extend, expand. If you only focus on earning money, you'll be broke. If you've worked most of your life, you've been making money. Just how much money throughout your life did you make? And how much did you save? Where is that money now? Whew! Tough questions. Questions no one wants to think about, but do it, then hurry along—we can't stay there.

The most important question is what are you going to do about it now. Right now! Are you ready to save more of your money? Are you ready to enlarge what you already have? Managing and showing good stewardship over your current funds will open the door to managing more, for, "Whoever can be trusted with very little can also be trusted with much, and whoever is dishonest with very little will also be dishonest with much (Luke 16:10 NIV)." This one area of commitment is a defining factor in your financial success.

"I'm not living large; I just want
to live comfortably.
I wanna have financial stability
that is unshakable."
Queen Latifah

How well is your money working for you?

Make One Financial Decision at a Time

When you first start digging and performing surgery on your finances, it can be overwhelming. You might even shed some excruciating tears. Cry. Get it out. When you see how much you owe or assess how you spent your money, it will pinch you in the back underneath your arm with a good ole twist! Ouch! But if you are committed to the task, you will accept the gift that you must unpack, and as mentioned earlier forgive yourself, and get to the business of the business: your finances.

What kinds of decisions will you need to make when deciding on how to manage your finances properly? Where should you start? Well, there are several categories to consider, such as:

- Increasing your cash flow,
- Budgeting,
- Paying off.debt,
- Saving for emergencies and future purchases,
- Investing (in assets),
- Retiring,
- Estate Planning,
- Protecting your assets, and yes,
- Improving your financial literacy.

To be effective, focus on one step at a time (except for the literacy part and even investing, those are simultaneous acts–time waits for no one, but it's best to be strategic about such tasks.).

When I first started with this "*getting my finances together*" shindig, I wasn't budgeting. I specifically focused on increasing my cash flow–both using the money I already made and trying to make more through side hustles. I just started! Afterwards, I began outlining small steps to focus on which decreases stress, helps you operate on strategy, keeps you focused, gives you a place to jump back in the game when and if you fall, and keeps you winning. Some items will take precedence like emergencies, taxes owed to the IRS, or keeping the car from getting repossessed, and other financial roadblocks that need attention a month ago. Don't let that overwhelm you. Focus on gaining control of one financial issue at a time. However, scaling your financial knowledge will be a dual benefi t to your goals.

Here are steps to help you get out of the Red Zone (overspending) and into the Green Zone (just right spending). These steps will help you ditch the stress of financial debt by allowing you to increase your C.A.S.H.F.L.O.W.. This model is not for the fast and furious. However, in our current economy of high inflation, then increased rates from the federal reserve, and recession, some of us need to get financially stronger sooner rather than later, myself included. I hold to the premise of keeping debt low in your personal finances (leverage debt using your business or as I've learned use other financial workarounds (like trusts), so you don't lose important assets that are vital to you and your family. Here I lobby for you to do the following:

Change Your Mindset

Attack EMOTIONAL Spending

Script a Budget

Hold Firm to the Emergency Fund

Fill YOUR Pockets

Level the Debt

Obtain Your Full Emergency Fund & Deeds

Welcome Wealth

Time to expound on each item in my C.A.S.H.F.L.O.W. model I have developed through my experiences, following my plans, and listening to experts in webinars or reading. It's a mixture of mindset, behavior, and money strategies. Most strategies I see get straight to the process, and your mindset, emotions, and behaviors are up to you to figure out. Believe it or not our money problems are more about behavior than money. The actions and inactions we make matter. It's drenched in what we believe and how we think–the perfect portrait of our manifestations. Building a solid foundation and financial confidence takes time.

Change Your Mindset

I have spent most of this book trying to help you de-stress and change your mindset. Hopefully, you're convinced by now that your mindset is the one treasure you possess to conquer every goal in your life. So, put aside your race, what's in your bank account, history with money, and current environment. The *only* blockers keeping you from building a better financial lifestyle is your mind. #BuildBackYourPersonalEconcomy

So let's build our money mindset.

1. Read different financial literacy books from different perspectives.
2. Follow and listen to established gurus on podcasts and social media platforms.
3. Take free financial literacy classes at church and non-profit community organizations. (Less selling here.)
4. Get a small group of serious and trusted friends to discuss money moves (saving, investing, budgeting, etc.).
5. Believers get rooted in what God says about money. Do this study for yourself in your devotional time.
6. Come to terms with your thoughts about money. They could be holding you back. #keepit100

So, what thoughts do you *really* have about money? Let's get real for a moment. Our childhood, past, and current ideologies about money go with us everywhere. Get clear on what you think about money and assess how it led us to your current situation.

So grab your journal, pen and get to writing.

Time to Write:

What do you believe about money?
Where do you spend the bulk of your money?
Who taught you about money growing up as a child? What did they teach you?
What did you learn about money in school? College?What money challenges have you had as an adult? How does money affect your relationships?
How do you feel when you have enough money? How do you feel when you don't have enough money?
If you've borrowed money before, how did it make you feel?
Are you able to talk openly about money? Why or why not?
Who can you talk to about money?
Honestly, how does it feel to talk about money?
Does your partner feel the same as you do about money?How important is money in your relationship?
Do you talk about money as a family?
Is it necessary to you that you leave an inheritance behind?
What are your thoughts and feelings surrounding debt? Do you carry a lot of debt? Why?
How much debt should people have?
What is good debt? What is bad debt?
Are you for or against student loans? Why?
Are you capable of teaching your kids or someone you know about money?
Do you feel you can give (without regrets) to others with your money situation?
How do you feel about others borrowing money from you?
Do you give to charity? How important is it to give money to others?

Does someone owe you money? How does that feel?
How does spending money make you feel? Why do you think it makes you feel this way?
Do you make enough money? Why or why not?
In what ways could you make more money?
Are you good with money?
Do you save money?
Do you have insurance? Why or why not? What types? Are you prepared to pay for your next emergency? Do you have an emergency fund?
How does money impact your physical health?
Do you have enough money to pay for health procedures?
What three things get in the way of you being financially stable?
Have you thought about retirement?
What will you use for retirement funds? What happens to your loved ones if you die? Will they have enough money to live comfortably?
How much do you know about taxes? Insurance? Retirement? Stocks? Bonds? Investment accounts?
Is credit good or bad?
When should you use a credit card?
How much money is enough money?
If you lost all of your money, what would you do?
How do you feel you should invest your money?
Do you have a financial advisor?
Is there someone helping you with your finances?How do you feel about working with financial experts? Who is the most financially responsible person you know? Would you like to be rich? Wealthy? Why? Define the difference.
How much money would you need to be rich? Wealthy?
What would you do with the money?
What are your money goals?
What does financial freedom or financial independence mean to you?

I asked a lot of questions so that you can reflect on your thoughts surrounded by money. As you can see, money topics are vast. We only know what we know until we get educated and learn more. I hope you take the time to answer them and discuss them with family and friends. Some of the questions are located at the end of the book.

Make Your Money

Graduating from high school, going to college, and getting a good-paying job are the way to financial stability. Sounds right to you? That's what we were fed. We were taught to get a job from the school system, our parents, and the government. Making money means you get a job and work for someone else. I cringe because that's not the *only* way!

And for most of my life, that was the notion I utilized. Though I had investments early on (as a teenager), I didn't view them as keenly as I should've. Yes, the money I had invested had grown; however, I failed to see my potential future—that investing is another way that I could make money (way above my paycheck). I invested more energy into my job with hard labor, than the *who, what, when, where,* and *why* of where I was investing my money.

My first *real life* introduction to investing was a stock club that a family friend's grandmother developed for us kids. I was eighteen or nineteen at the time with two other friends, one of which I was her personal aide. We called ourselves *The Ladybugs*. Granny put $50 in our accounts every month for two or three years. Every two to three months, we would meet up to research and invest our money in companies we were familiar with and liked. I remember we bought stock shares in Disney (before it split into Pixar), Johnson and Johnson, National Beverage Corporation, Centerpoint Energy, Bayer, Starbucks, and a few others in 2000-2001.

We agreed that we had to hold the money in the account for at least three years, which was easy for us because we were young and didn't have a full understanding of investing. I didn't understand the value of those lessons until more recently. I didn't see the big picture until it was too late. I sold many of those stocks during times of *need*, or so I thought; more like times of poor money management. As I look back on some of the positions I held, many companies paid dividends quarterly, and are notorious in their lane of brilliance today.

So not only was I making money as the stocks rose in value, I would get additional profits from dividend payments that were reinvested to buy more stock. I still have that account and plan to grow it to live off the dividends, making Granny proud that she taught me the basics of investing. I never knew how blessed I was, and now I know my money journey has led me to this point in life.

Another way to make money is to start a business. Why weren't there any classes on that? I remember the first product I ever sold as a youngin' in middle school. I made a San Francisco 49ers pillow in home economics class. At the time, my principal wanted to buy the pillow because that was his favorite team. I don't remember what I charged him, but I know I got suckered into accepting a low price (I remember wishing I'd charged more like $20.00). But hey, as a kid, I made some money. That experience didn't quite stick (making a product and selling it), but I continued looking for entrepreneurship opportunities over the years as an adult.

I tried to sell make-up, jewelry, energy, did photography (sometimes I still do), started a cookie business (more recent), multi-level marketing, and babysat during high school. I'm not a salesperson, but I was not a stranger to being a *trypreneur*, as some say (lol)! I didn't quite have all the mechanics down to what makes a business at those times, so I gave up and kept trying. Even though I could see the benefits on my tax returns, I did not have many of the puzzle pieces until a few years before writing this book. To be in business is a considerable tax benefit! People don't understand the advantages they are missing out on by having side hustles–we focus on the money we make now, instead of the many advantages that we get by keeping good records, tracking expenses, and meeting with professionals (more on business later). Business is a great way to make money upfront and on the back-end of the tax system.

We make money by getting a job, investing, and starting a business or side hustle (whichever you'd like to call it). These are the basics. Each of these has a slew of subcategories on how to make money. Some alternate legal ways include contracting your skills, selling your plasma, garage sales, buying real estate, renting our cars and spaces, taking surveys, or using coupon apps. You can make money with your labor, but find ways to make money while you're sleeping too. There are unlimited ways to increase your cash flow, and the internet has expanded that notion.

We all have the capacity to make money. We have to change our mindset about what we can do. However, making and having more money is not the problem with most Americans. We, unfortunately, live beyond our means. Spending less than what you make *still* works. It is not outdated; it's a foundation along with paying yourself first.

People argue with me today that debt is good, and we can learn to live with it. *I can't deal with y'all!* If you have seen the stench of debt first hand and the tragedies I've witnessed, you'd be cautious with the average person carrying so much debt.

Real talk: we can make all the money we want, but if we don't wrap our minds and behaviors in a solid foundation with managing it, protecting it, and investing it, we'll find ourselves light years behind those who do. The wealth gap will get bigger, and we'll still raise our fist at the government. Look around: who's truly responsible for your circumstance? When you change your mind, you change your money.

The Education System

Now think back: What did you learn in school about money? You were in school for at least 12-13 years—the place where they taught you what you needed to know to be holistically successful in our society—our capitalistic society. What did your K-12 education teach you about money (it will differ for us all)? And let's take it one step further: What did your college degree teach you about money? There's a high percentage of people walking across college stages with diplomas and debt! What is the education system *truly* doing?

When I think back to those moments, K-12 taught me the basics of money, counting money, and minor accounting tasks. I recall completing a project about the stock market in twelfth grade. Then, during my college years, I got plenty of credit cards (on school grounds) with free T-shirts and even signed a bunch of promissory notes (student loans) that I have paid for exponentially. When I look back on it all, I learned to continue the cycle of debt in this country. What puts the sprinkles on the cookie for me is finding out that graduates with business and finance degrees leave without some of the most basic money principles that wealthy people use daily. EVERY DAY! You shouldn't be ashamed of your lack of knowledge: You only know what you know until you know more—but we can all thank a system that teaches you more about how to spend than save.

There are many questions to ask regarding finances and a plethora of vehicles and obstacles created by our legislative system that will snatch money right out of your paychecks or accounts before you can blink. Others will grant you the peace to keep more of your money—the money you work hard to earn.

If you were never taught the rules of the game, can you succeed? No one wants to play Spades with someone who doesn't know how to play unless they're on the opposing team! Seriously, you can't be my partner! LOL! How simple is it to run game on people who are blind and naive—naive to the fact that big business, government, banks, and creditors don't have their best interest?

Some of us grew up and received viable information about finances, while others got crumbs of financial education here and there. During my senior year of high school, I had a half-semester economics course with a New York Stock Exchange (NYSE) project (OK, I'm a little bitter y'all!). Notice, the class was HALF A SEMESTER! People become millionaires using the stock market! Why not give students a longer (like four years) and more in-depth economics study without the fluffy stuff? It deserves that amount of attention because our personal economies are what we have to navigate for most of our lives.

Schools should teach what we need to know to live beyond high school to a higher degree. Thankfully, the pandemic sparked institutions, parents, and people to develop more financial literacy programs for our youth and young adults. There have been huge initiatives from big named celebrities, financial gurus, and financial institutions that have partnered with schools and communities to educate the masses.

During my years growing up, most schools incorporated many theories and basic life skills on balancing a checkbook, economics, and how to add and subtract dollars and cents to help students. But unless you took a finance class (if your school offered one), like personal finance, or accounting (I took one), or home economics (which schools have been slowly filtering out), or had decent parental guidance, you started wavelengths behind your counterparts. And let's not discuss the wealth gaps due to racial inequality!

Furthermore, how many of us were warned about the bankers on college campuses handing out credit cards to first-year students (all students really) without jobs? Part of The Credit Card Act of 2009 helped with such practices. Before such laws, however, I got my fair share of T-shirts, pens, beer-opening key chains, and koozies in exchange for my information and an approved amount of debt! So much debt! And I know plenty of people who can relate. However, college affiliations with banks and credit card companies still exist, some with great intentions of educating students. Think: *Is the debt going down, though?* Why are college students targeted? And what should we do about it?

We need to challenge our schools to emphasize financial literacy in our K-12 programs and undergraduate degrees. (*With all due respect, parents and adults with kids in your lives need to teach your children as well.*) There's no way college students should be entering and leaving college without knowing basic information about finances: bank account options, budgeting, emergency funds, taxes, insurance options, credit education, buying a car, effectively investing in the stock market, starting a business, other investment options, retirement accounts, savings and municipal bonds, certificates of deposit, the purpose of the W4 and how to fill it out, purchasing a house, etc. There are many more topics, but basic information is needed (enough to spark interest) about many of these topics. You can't tell me we can't find a way to put Personal Finances 101 and 102 in the first two years.

And yes, we *all* know we can find this information online now. However, educational institutions must emphasize niche financial topics, or students won't know to look it up,—unless of course, they have a keen sense of curiosity.

Everything must be taught in context, but (I repeat) for a college student (who's paid THOUSANDS OF DOLLARS) to leave or start college without some of these essential items mentioned above is quite upsetting. I have spoken to many adults who attest to being frustrated while trying to figure out their finances, even choosing the right benefits during open enrollment on their jobs. Adults trying to be adults.

Our education **must** start at home when the systems are not in place to educate our citizens. Growing up with parents as financial mentors is a better start to life in America than those who don't. It doesn't take a finance degree to teach your kids, but it does take some knowledge and skill to impart valuable money lessons. Start with what you know, research, ask questions, and invest in expert advice for the rest. You probably have friends who are bankers, economists, auditors, collection agents, etc., who could impart some wisdom. Ask your questions and relay the message to your family. Don't wait on the government. We must educate ourselves and the next generation to combat a flawed system that is behind in educating its constituents (all of us).

Money is a Tool

One rule you need to come to terms with is that money is a tool—it's a resource. It should not sit under a mattress or hide under the earth with a treasure map in a deposit box (lol!). It is a tool to be utilized for us to live, uplift, build, destroy barriers, and grow. We cannot take it with us when we depart from our bodies. Neither should it slip through our hands like the chaff from the wheat. We must use it responsibly because it plays a vital role in our lives and everyone around us. Note: not every tool fixes every problem. So, money is a tool to improve specific matters, but we know it can't fix everything.

Money in the Bible. These principles can be found throughout the Bible as well. Several verses show how God wants wealth for His people, "There should be no poor among you," and "you will lend to many nations, but borrow from none," "At the end of every seven years you must cancel debts. (Deuteronomy 15:1, 4, 6; 28:12 NIV)." This text is in reference to Jewish people, but that promise extended to Gentiles through Jesus! Over and over, the Word tells you to use money, not hoard it and keep it for oneself, but to grow it and bless others, especially your fellow brothers and sisters in Christ! He gives you the ability to produce wealth (Deuteronomy 8:18), but if you try to hold on to it, you will surely lose it, for "one person gives freely, yet gains even more; another withholds unduly, but comes to poverty (Proverbs 11:24 NIV)." We have a Christian obligation to utilize the resources God has given us appropriately.

I remember a time when I did not understand the parable about the talents in the Bible. I didn't understand why the servant who saved the money was admonished. Check it out in Matthew 25: A Master gave three of his servants varying numbers of talents. One multiplied the talent by a lot, another by a little, and another none at all because he hid the *talents* in the ground, saying that he found that his Master was shrewd, often reaping where he didn't sew. The Master got upset, saying, "You should've at least deposited it into the bank so it could earn interest." In other words, to let it sit and rot was not putting it to best use. In my mind (before I understood this), I was like, "Why can't he just save it?" like seriously, what's wrong with that? I get multiple messages here about us utilizing the talents (our gifts and money) God gave us to fulfill the commission, being fruitful, and good stewards. Still, we can learn a lesson that our money shouldn't be sitting in the ground, unbothered and rotting away. We should make good use of our money. Don't waste your "talents" or natural abilities (your God-given gifts) or money on things that will rot; try putting them in assets that grow, so you can use it for kingdom building and the building up of others. At the end of the day, I want to say I used my resources well, that I wasn't stingy, and I took care of the my family and the poor, putting my faith in action–"Thy good and faithful servant."

Therefore, we should place our money where it will earn higher interest than a regular savings account. For example, you may think about utilizing a money market account (MMA), high-yield savings account (HYSA) which is not too high during the writing of this book, or another vehicle (bonds, real estate, etc.) to earn higher returns on your money. Where you put it depends on your risk level and intentions for your funds (easily liquidated for emergencies or hold long-term).

Continue to wrap your head around the idea that money is a tool. It can help you bless others, send someone off to college, live in a safer place with more opportunities, put you around the right people, help you lobby for your ideas, or put you or someone you trust in a position of influence. We don't always use it for the right reasons, but if you keep in mind that it's a resource for you to grow, you'll be thinking along the right lines.

Think: How can you use the money that comes through your hands as a tool? You can't get control of anything that you can't hold on to nor desire to spend it before you even make it. Settle this one theory and make it a daily habit to say: Money is a tool. In what ways will you use it to build?

Say: Money is a tool. How I use it determines my outcomes.

Manage Your Money

Minimize your Taxes

"In America, there are two tax systems, one for the informed and one for the uniformed. Both are legal."
Judge Learned Hand

Now that we have it down, money is a tool; we again have to shift our thinking about taxes! We have got to STOP handing out free money! Do you know the IRS reports that most people overpay their taxes each year? Overpay taxes? Yes, OVERPAY! This is the one area that people, *my people, American people,* need to understand, so I'm placing taxes under "Change Your Mindset" because you have to make a shift in your thinking to get your money now and not later. Taxes are our greatest expense (and interest). And most consumers know very little about the subject, except to pay taxes, don't mess with the IRS, and move on. #metoo

There are a different set of rules, however, when it comes to taxes. There are rules for employees and rules for business owners.

Employees! *Stop* giving the government an interest-free loan every paycheck and *start* restructuring what's coming out of your check. Are you looking at your paycheck stubs? Do you see the amount of taxes that you're allowing the government to take? It's rough, but read all the details you're missing out on when you only focus on what's in your hand. You're missing your tax dollars you're paying every week. That should motivate you and prompt you to start asking why and how can you minimize those taxes? You work too hard to be looking for the work you did today, last week, or two weeks ago to be given back to you twelve or more months later.

Small Business Owners! You, too, need to stop giving the government your hard-earned dollars! I'm talking to myself too. Make sure your business is legit and keep good records: Keep your receipts and document all your transactions (hire the right professionals to manage your accounting and taxes). Rewards are for those who are informed and well-documented. Most business owners lose out because we don't keep good records and hire appropriate tax professionals (#guilty). If you don't know enough, you'll hire anyone. But when you're informed, you can ask the right questions to understand if the professional is right for you. How much money are you leaving on the table by not consulting with the pros?

The wealthy are always looking for ways to minimize their taxes. That's right! They are LOOKING for ways to avoid their tax obligation and save more of their money.

Tax avoidance is LEGAL.

Tax evasion is ILLEGAL.

First, there are tax laws for employees and tax laws for businesses. Employees pay the highest taxes because LABOR is taxed more in a capitalistic society. You work, you're taxed, and then you are paid. A business owner works, gets paid, and pays taxes last (however, there are quarterly taxes that should be paid).

The fact that businesses have more deductible expenses can make their taxable income much lower than their employees. Giant corporations can end up paying little to zero in federal taxes because they have superior accounting departments to manage their financial transactions and strategize their moves (*umm, you can too*: *hire a tax pro*)! Sure, they pay other business taxes, but they have an opportunity to pay less in federal income taxes, which take a healthy portion from hard-working citizens. Some companies even get a rebate: Yes, they get money from the government! Search: "*2018 company pays zero taxes receives millions*" and see which company paid zero dollars in federal taxes on billions of dollars in profit but received over $100 million in return. Amazing, amazing! There are other Fortune 500 companies that pay little to zero dollars in federal taxes. It pays to have a business.

Did you look it up?

You BIG MAD or LITTLE MAD? Heck, if you're not asking yourself how you can do this too, we are not cut from the same cloth! We all have the same opportunity to decrease the amount of taxes we pay. However, when I asked social media (in a group of 1.8 million members) if they were getting their tax money upfront, most people were on opposite ends: either too scared or making sure they don't pay one penny more. Look, I get it. No one wants to owe or pay penalties. However, we can get a tax expert and make sure we're paying the **correct amount**. Meet. Plan. Strategize. It's doable. *Who's better at spending your money: the government or you?*

Why do the wealthy get all the deductions? Great question: because those persons and organizations are ALWAYS looking for ways to minimize their taxes (and the laws are on the side of those who take risks; business owners). Personal opinion here: they pay attention to elections, propositions, and the political arena, making sure to support who'd benefit them the most. Many of my people haven't been paying attention. We're too busy surviving otherwise we'd know certain "tax companies" work alongside the government to keep more of your money. Let me *hursh*. You'd find the deductions too if you were looking for them, knew about them, were in the right circle of people, or consulted with professionals. The wealthy put their money into investments (i.e. hedge funds, stocks, opportunities, etc.) and assets that make money for them, which are tax deductible, tax deferred, or tax free.

Simultaneously, many of us are still OVERPAYING, and celebrating our *refunds*, not *rebates*! So many people are sleeping on the W-4 as a strategy. They've completed it once (when hired) and kept it moving. And many people still try to hold on and do their own taxes without a professional tax expert, which is another way we overpay by *leaving money on the table*. Get *all* of your coins! That doesn't mean you can't prepare your taxes, but have an expert look it over before you file. It's their duty to keep up with the laws that help their customers save money!

Homework: 1. Find out how much you're paying in taxes on your paycheck. 2. Search to find out the top businesses that paid zero federal tax dollars in previous years. If those companies, who make trillions, billions, and millions aren't paying federal taxes, why are you overpaying? Let's use the law to our advantage too.

I'm paying ______________________________ in federal taxes each paycheck. A few major companies paying zero dollars in federal taxes are:

____

I (am/ am not) overpaying taxes because: (If you get a ***refund (not rebate)*** back you're overpaying.)

____

____

List a few beneficial ways you could use the tax money that's coming out of your paycheck.

____

____

If you were to get some of this money back would you put it to good use? Be honest. It's easy to fall right back into the same money traps.

____

Now, how can we minimize our tax obligation?

The first step in minimizing your taxes as an employee is to correct your W-4 form. This form tells your job exactly how much to take out of your paycheck! Yes, I know most people have not even looked at their W-4 since they started working at their job. Let's back up.

Who taught you how to fill out the W-4? Just think back. Can't remember? Maybe someone told you what to write but never explained the actual purpose of the document. If you are blessed, a parent, significant other, boss/coworker, or your savviness in looking it up, guided you through the process. Most of us either put a 0 or a 1 for ourselves, then gradually added dependents or never went back to update our dependents.

You may find that your human resource department will generally assist you. HR representatives are cautious with this form, as they can be held responsible (possibly sued) for wrong information. The level of help you may get here may vary as they can help, but cannot give you advice. But don't let that stop you from asking: there are plenty of knowledgeable and helpful HR representatives.

Everyone's scared of the IRS (*except when it comes to adding other people's kids to their tax return*, #isaidit). Trust me, I was scared to correct my W-4 as well. I played it safe. Originally, I was paying almost $200 a paycheck in Federal Taxes. Once I corrected it (*modestly*), my contributions decreased about $45. Then, I corrected it again in 2020 (with Enrolled Agents), and got an extra $85. I still pay taxes; however, now, I pay the **correct amount**.

2019

STATEMENT OF EARNINGS AND DEDUCTIONS -PLEASE DE

Earnings	Hours	Amount	Deductions	Amount
SALARY		$1875.34	MEDICARE	34.64
			FED TAX	152.47
			TRS*	193.17
			TRS CARE	16.31

2020

STATEMENT OF EARNINGS AND DEDUCTIONS -PLEASE DE

Earnings	Hours	Amount	Deductions	Amount
SALARY		$1950.27	MEDICARE	35.25
			FED TAX	67.59
			TRS*	198.89
			TRS CARE	16.79

An altered version of my paycheck statement.

At least now, we have the good ol' internet, and you can search for "How to fill out my W-4" or use the withholding estimator from the IRS. At least, get educated about what to do. However, my suggestion is to hire an Enrolled Agent of the IRS who can help you fill out this form based on your specific situation. It does zero good to correct the W-4 however, and waste the money—why mindset is important.

* * *

Have you ever read the entire document? To fully understand the W-4 form, you need to read the entire document. If not, I encourage you to do so. You can find the entire four-page document on the IRS website (https://www.irs.gov/pub/irs-pdf/fw4.pdf) or go to www.thecashflowconvo.com and look under resources.

And to be embarrassingly transparent, I read the entire document with the help of a business partner, Henry A. Reid, a few years before this publication. Here I am in my late 30s with two degrees behind my name, an educator, and I had NEV-ER read the W-4 form in its entirety nor understood its entire purpose. What a blow to the ego, right? I knew it took out taxes, but there were bits and pieces of information I missed. Do you know how hard that hit me? I started telling EVERYBODY! And I mean everybody! Some people looked at me like, okay, yeah, I know. And I'm looking around like, why didn't someone tell me? Like, I've been doing life all wrong!

Have I even lived (LOL)!

Again, the purpose of a W-4 is to control the taxes that come out of your paycheck. Your goal should be to pay the right amount of taxes so you do not owe the IRS at the end of the year—this is contradictory to what *many* people have become accustomed to. We should NOT be looking to get a REFUND. A refund means that you overpaid. Yes, that's right, overpaid! Your goal should be to balance out at $0.00 or get a rebate.

At least now, the old days of putting a 0 or a 1 are over. The IRS has "simplified" its W-4 form, including a calculator which shows the amount of taxes withheld from your paycheck. This form continues to change over time. But at the time of this writing, it's easier to see what you're overpaying with the new withholdings estimator (**STOP**: and see my example in the bonus material). When the results show you exactly how much you're OVERPAYING, a lightbulb should go oĀ in your head. Come to the light, I say!

Side note: Do an internet search for ***the IRS withholding calculator*** to find the estimator (https://apps.irs.gov/app/tax-withholding-estimator) or visit www.thecashflowconvo.com.

The Skeptics: You mean I'm not going to get a lump sum of money from the government next year?

Me: You were NEVER getting money from the government; it's YOUR money. You're getting your money back. That's it. It's YOUR MO-NEY!

Just think about what you could have paid for or how many opportunities you could've taken advantage of if you had your money every month and not just once a year? On average, that's an extra $200-$500 a month that goes out the door to the government. The *ripe* amount to crush your debt!

Can we say FREE LOAN?

That's right! When you overpay your taxes, you give the government a free loan, meaning you don't charge them interest for lending them your money. When was the last time you received a free loan, without interest, for twelve months or more? Legally!

Now that your money is on hold, what is the government doing with it: .

- Approving student loans
- Paying for Government contracts
- Making money from your money
- Loaning or giving it out to business owners,
- foreign aid to other countries
- and more knowns and unknowns!

Imagine that: You have helped other people in other countries AND sent someone's child to school! You can view it as a good or bad act, but who's *still* missing out all year round?

Meanwhile, back in Stressville, about ⅓ of your paycheck is missing, your bills are non-stop, getting out of debt seems like a lifetime away, you're living paycheck to paycheck, and you're using credit cards, payday loans, title loans, pawning items, and borrowing from family and friends to get by. That's the *pie in the sky living* my brother always talks about—I feel you, bro! We are meant to thrive on this side of life too.

When you *actually* get *some* of the money back the following year, you're catching up on old bills or trying to treat yourself, and thus, the cycle begins again. Most of us know someone that fits this category, and many of us have been there ourselves. There's no doubt WE NEED TO BREAK THIS CYCLE!

As a start, update your W-4 form anytime you have a major life change, such as getting married, divorced, having children, adding dependents, a death, starting a business, or tax law changes. For example, significant changes took place to the tax laws in 2018, but most people did not update their W-4 (neither did I because I didn't know). It's good practice to take a look at this document at the beginning of the new year (changes were made for 2021, too! I got the warning from my HR department, did you?)

Instead of getting your money back annually, aim to get the **correct** amount each paycheck, each month. Remember those paycheck stubs we just looked at? Well, how much are they taking out? Could you use a few hundred from that amount each month (to ditch debt or invest)? For most people, an extra $500 would help them get out of debt and stop living paycheck to paycheck. That's $6,000 a year towards debts, investments, or opportunities—a chance to buy assets and not liabilities!

People need to pay the taxes in our society, but overpaying creates problems for millions of people.

"The rich and wealthy are always looking for ways to minimize their taxes."

You can legally avoid paying too much in taxes by using tax strategies and looking to put your money into accounts that are tax-deductible, tax-deferred, or tax-free (aka tax-advantage) investments. So that means the money you put into such accounts can **lower your taxable income**. Taxable income is the taxes you owe to the government when you make money (from all sources).

One way to take advantage of tax-deductible opportunities is to invest in business ventures because businesses help lower your taxable income. And with the right company, such as a home-based business, you can deduct expenses you're already using to lower your taxable income. I advocate for a home-based business because there are many tax deductions you can take advantage of that you're already paying for today. I did it selling jewelry, photography, energy, make-up, and cookies.

Don't get it twisted, however: Businesses still pay a healthy share of taxes, but they also get greater incentives under the law. Business expenses can include rent/mortgage, mileage, home office expenses, internet, cell phone bill, utilities, eating out, and hundreds more! They are eligible for grants and loans with premium terms.

Oh, don't let me forget paying your employees: aka your kids. Now that's one strategy you don't want to miss! Do some homework and research "*how to hire your kids*." Your home is the primary place to begin because you're already paying for the space. Many businesses start at home, and the tax advantages are lucrative. Your business does not have to be grand. It could be small and quaint, enough to satisfy your needs. A little-known truth: people can pass down their business, but they can't pass down their jobs to their loved ones. You can pass down your debt, but you can't pass down that paycheck. It's no wonder that the *wealth that sticks* is inside the family. Look at your clothes, television networks, food companies, electricity entities, restaurants, etc., that have been around for a century or more. Which companies have lasted from generation to generation that you know? Wouldn't you like to create a legacy of your own?

If you're already a business owner:

Other ways to lower your taxes. Make sure you apply all the tax credits and deductions applicable to you. How will you know? You don't if you're not keeping up with the laws. I'll say it several more times in this chapter: hire a tax expert to help you. These individuals study the laws that change each year. Get a good tax accountant or enrolled agent, whether you're an employee or business owner. A preparer is not always an expert, and many do not have the credentials comparable to a tax accountant who plans. I am not suggesting that *all* preparers are not informed as some do a great job, have to go through extensive training, and have been helping people for years. On the other hand, I did my taxes all my life until I ran into my own tax problem. I was overwhelmed and frankly still am (lol)! Luckily I started learning *the mistakes I made* because I was still planning on doing them after procrastinating for several years. Once I realized I was leaving money on the table, I found a tax professional *pronto*–which is a journey in itself. I was penny-pinching, not wanting to give up one dime. I cringed at paying $100 or more for tax software! I saved myself time and money by letting experts do what they do best. Ching-ching! As long as your actions are legal, ethical, and moral, you deserve to keep more money in YOUR pocket.

Your money is waiting for you to take control and manage it strategically! With that said, I hope you decide today that you will not overpay your taxes and that you will find a knowledgeable tax expert, solicit help to **update** your W-4 form for the current year, and get the tax credits, deductions, and benefits that the law says you can. You deserve it!

Off the cuff: Make sure you interview the person doing your taxes. Everyone is not qualified to give you the best experience. You want someone to work hard for you. Choose quality first and not convenience. If they're going to provide you with a rapid refund (AND TAKE MORE OF YOUR MONEY), it's a scam, in my opinion. Tax preparation is a billion-dollar business. That's BILLION! (So much so that top tax software companies lobby to keep the tax return process convoluted for Americans.) And people get robbed out of their hard-earned dollars and never question it. They'll quickly give up $2,000 to get $4,000 in their pockets as soon as possible. Stop throwing your money away. Look around your neighborhood and see all the ways you are being taken advantage of for your *after-tax dollars*: check cashing, payday loans, rental wheel services, title loans, rent to buy stores, and rapid tax refund places—strategically set in *certain* neighborhoods. Let's avoid being hoodwinked or fall for the "okie doke," as I say. Every brick-and-mortar business searches for the right location before laying ground. Your neighborhood was targeted. Be wiser with your money.

Everyone has a plan for your money. Do you?

Attack Emotional Spending and Break Up with Money

Most of us do it, have done it, and will do it—make a future emotional purchase, that is. Let's face it: When it comes to money, we get deep in our feelings. It's an invasive topic. But what *is* **emotional spending**? And how do you stop it? When you make financial transactions and decisions solely because you are sad, angry, vindictive, *feel* obligated (feel guilty), grieving, elated, depressed, furious, afraid, pressured, giddy, and egotistical, you're spending emotionally. We often *need* these items at the time to self-pacify, numb, prove a point, "get someone off our backs." or reward ourselves. "Well, hmm, I don't do that. I'm very systematic in how I spend money." Are you sure? Let's see if any of the following hits home.

What does emotional spending look like? Check off any that apply to you.

_____ Buying the newest (gaming system, phone update, kicks, car, technology, etc.) because you have to have the new-new!
_____ Shopping without intention (*I'll get what speaks to me*).
_____ Shopping because it makes you feel good to have new things.
_____ Impressing someone on a date.
_____ Putting more than you planned in the church collection because you feel guilty (2 Corinthians 9:7).
_____ Buying items for your child because you didn't get a lot when you were a child.
_____ Giving money to a *friend* who always needs *your* help (feel obligated).
_____ Bailing someone out of trouble (repeatedly) because you can't say *no*.
_____ Overbuying during Black Friday. You want it but don't have the money.
_____ Spending more than you have on Christmas because you can't let others down.
_____ You buy food to celebrate or numb dissatisfaction.
_____ Paying for all the drinks at the bar to look good or gain points in the eyes of others.
_____ Buying a gift for office celebrations because everyone else is doing it, and you would hate to be the odd one out.
_____ Purchasing from your friend's new business venture, even when you can't afford to.
_____ Gambling.
_____ Booking trips to get away from negativity and clear your head.
_____ Buying anything to impress others (house, cars, clothes, red bottoms, J's, grills, etc.)
_____ Spending money because someone begged you to do this or that with them (i.e. trip, events)

_____ Getting tattoos, piercings, new hairstyles after a breakup.

_____ Buying things to suppress feelings and thoughts or to get away.

_____ Buying a house (or car) because you want to look the part (not be embarrassed).

_____ Supporting family members because you feel obligated to help each time they get into trouble (the pressure is real).

_____ Spending money carelessly after bad news.

_____ Buying elaborate gifts (or any gift) to outdo others.

______ Choosing to attend the "better school" because it's a name-brand university instead of a local community college.

_____ Purchasing items in the name of "I deserve..." or "I'm entitled to..." because I did this...or that.... (Look around: You're not the only one who jumped over a hurdle or two. Focus on your goals and don't go overboard.)

Write your own: ______________________________

____

Basically, for many statements above: *I gotta have it syndrome*. Who else is guilty? Don't leave me hanging! I know you've done it, and we will do it again. At least this time, you can be a little more fiscal when you do.

We could go on, but I think you get the picture. Many experiences can trigger emotional spending: Mental health issues, breakups/divorce, death, job loss, career competitiveness, addictions, depression, low self-esteem or self-efficacy, dating, excitability, harsh constructive criticism or criticism, peer-pressure, guilt, overworked, feeling excluded, medical diagnosis, new relationship, a promotion, holidays, sales, or a PANDEMIC! Just about anything can cause someone to spend emotionally. However, it's time to break up with your money and attack the spending.

Dear Ben,

It's not you; it's me....

Yours Truly,

Humans are emotional beings, so, naturally, we spend because of our emotions. If unchecked, however, many of our actions can become knee-jerk reactions wrapped in illogical decision-making. With thousands of dollars in emotional transactions, what should we do? It takes very little time to get into a financial pickle and decades (*even a lifetime*) to get out. Attack the emotional spending and break up with money.

We can't take out all of the emotions that come with spending, but we can be more conscious of how we spend. Most of our financial decisions should be logical, not emotional. We need to be more strategic in what we do. Planning for a specific amount of *play money* is better than having zero boundaries for your money. Pledge to grow your money, graciously give to others, and save more of your money. You cannot accomplish such tasks with emotionally derived decisions.

How are you spending your money?

To find out if you're emotionally spending, go back to the checklist above and the first chapter under *Check Yourself*. How does money make you feel? Is spending money the only way you know how to reward yourself? Do you spend money to escape? Do you have to spend money when you know it's in your account? How do you feel when you don't have money or cannot spend it to cover a bill? Do you buy impulsively? Do you shop to feel good? Do you have to hide your purchases or take them back? Do you overspend (I used to overspend by several hundred dollars each month. How is that possible?)? Do you feel better after spending? Feel guilty after spending?

I know that I still spend a surmountable amount of money eating out purely because I don't want to cook (#singlelifestruggles). However, when I plan my meals and have a set sum of money for eating out, it's better for my finances and even better for my health. That's my biggest vice, so I know exactly where to cut my spending in an effort to crush my goals.

Take some serious time to evaluate the questions, answer them, and figure out if you're an emotional spender. It'll save you a lot of headaches down the road. You need to be aware of your habits before you proceed to build a budget and master your finances.

My Emotional Spending Assessment

When I get money in my hands, I ______________________

____

When I don't have enough money, I ________________

____

____

I make emotional purchases when I am ______________

____

____

To curb my emotional spending, I will ______________

____

____

How can you avoid heartfelt, gut-wrenching, grief-ridden, and guilty purchases?

1. **Unsubscribe** to advertising in your email inbox, text messages, notifications, and social media accounts (unfollow). Tame your exposure to these outlets. Don't click on the links and scroll past the ads on social media. Don't entertain them at all. One text from your favorite store having a discount could send you spiraling.

2. **Budget**. Wahh, wahhh, waaaaahhh! Many people have a hard time accepting this, but you need a budget! Who cares if it's not natural (people argue this notion)! You will have more power and control over your finances. It's a right to spend money! We all like being in control (in various ways), right? Besides, you can build a little careless spending into your budget until you find that you don't need that category. When you finally understand (lightbulb moment), it could serve a better purpose. There are levels to this!
3. **Say *no*** to things, friends, and family who entice you (like the home buying parties or mall kiosks for items you don't need). Avoid peer pressure and limit your exposure to them. I always say, "*The world will teach you how to get into debt. Your family and friends will encourage your debt. And the creditors will profit from your debt until you have the courage to say NO.*" Say *no* to anything that is beyond your budget.
4. **Shape your world**. Put yourself around family and friends who understand your goals. Hang out in environments and people that will enhance your new goals. Maybe that's doing more home gatherings, finding free events, joining social media groups about living debt-free, finding free workshops from financial companies you already have established accounts with, or joining a book club. I reiterate: avoid temptations at all costs during the beginning stages. Until your "*no*" is firm, shape your environment until it becomes your routine. Then, traveling or going out with friends will be easier because you will have built up the stamina and a budget to avoid such spending.
5. **Seek professional help** if you cannot get things under control by yourself. Especially, if you have an addiction to gambling or spending in general. It

would be best if you got to the root of the problem. Consider a financial coach or, if your problem is rooted in deeper issues, go to therapy. Permit yourself to let others help you along the way.

6. **Journaling** is always a great way to work through problems. Write it down.
7. **Plan no-spending days**. Limit yourself to how many times you spend a month. Make it fun and be proud of yourself when you accomplish the goal.
8. **Keep yourself busy**. If you know you shop a lot when you're bored or because you're off, plan something on those days. Do something (volunteer, a hobby, gather with friends, exercise, etc.) better with your time.
9. **Deny access** to your money or lack thereof. Cut up the credit cards. Limit yourself to spending by denying access to cash and credit. Put your funds in an account (different bank) that causes you to go into the bank or takes several days to transfer to your regular account. Making your money harder to liquidate will help you in the long run.
10. **Be honest** with a partner or friend, who is good with money, about your spending habits. Be upfront about your highs and lows when it comes to spending, and be open to listening to your accountability partner for changes you need to make.

How excited are you to get started? Imagine how much better you will feel when you are not making emotionally stimulated decisions. Some of our most enormous debts come from heartfelt spending (*hello* to my piano), and we make them around important times in our lives like weddings, graduations, celebrations, near-death experiences, mid-life crises, birthdays, and holidays. How many people are still paying for Black Friday shopping? How many marriages have years of debt well into their marriage? Heck, sometimes the debt outlasts the marriage (sad face)! I paid off debts that I know I accrued years ago (emotionally spending) throughout writing this book. Let's see, I shopped during the 2017 Black Friday event and paid off the card in 2020 (*say what! exactly!)* and a timeshare in 2021 (#JesusTakeTheWheel)! I cringe just thinking about how many times I paid for STUFF due to interest and how much usage and joy they are bringing to date. I'm glad I broke up with spending and decided to move to a more stress-free way of living with money.

Breakups are complicated, and it takes some time to get used to tracking your money, so breathe. You will get better when you remain conscious of your spending habits and utilize a budget. Remember, distractions will come, but you have to be stronger than the situation and act on your vision—see the outcome. Attack your emotional spending and break up with money, so you can experience your breakthrough. I'm rooting for you!

Script a Budget

Remember when I said write it down? Now, it's time to script how you will spend your money. Stay with me: Most people will freak out at this point! I know: If you're not good with money, you *definitely* don't want to be tied to a budget. Why? Because you have a problem with bound-a-ries! If you are screaming, squinting, or squirming in your seat when you hear "*make a budget,*" it could be because you don't want to be *tied* down. You may feel claustrophobic. Or, I tried it, but it didn't work (*nothing works when you quit and embrace it with negativity).* I need you to think about the budget being empowering, enlightening, and elevating. Imagine having the power to say "*no*" to loved ones because it *ain't* in the budget, and saying "*yes*" to your favorite kicks or mini vacays, giving to an organization, financing a passion project, or fund a startup business because it *is* in the budget! NO GUILT trips here!

The only budget that will work is the one you script, the one you'll follow, the one you see through (#No*QuittersHere*). You cannot set a budget so strict that you're cheating on day three. You have to allow for your personal needs and *some* wants. At the same time, you have to have enough grit and sacrifice to say *no* to some extraneous expenses! Besides, you can't get to your goal without giving up something. Whatever habits you had groomed you for debt. Whatever mindset you have keeps you in debt and stressed. The goals you lack have you running in hexagons. (Lol, yeah, I said it!) You cannot keep those same habits to get yourself out of debt and out of stress—*Somethin's gotta change*.

Up until now, you may have been spending emotionally and all over the place, not knowing where your money is going, aiming at the wind, and coming up short at times. We stop that today. **I said**: We STOP that today (in my Deebo voice).

REPEAT (say it aloud): *I'm stopping that today. I'm going to be strategic about where my money goes. I rule the money; the money doesn't rule me. Therefore, I will spend the necessary time making, reviewing, and revamping my budget as needed, as often as I need to.*

Did you say it with assertion? Go back and say it in a more convincing way to yourself. Write it on a sticky note and place it in a frequently visited place. Then tell a quality person in your life. Call them up and tell them; be accountable. This step is essential if you lack grit. Some of us work jobs in which the money is not consistent. Some of us will have to pay ahead due to the inconsistent checks, while others take home the same pay every two weeks. You see the struggle. You *gotta* be committed.

We are all dealing with different situations. The beauty of the budget is that it pinpoints where your money will go. This way, instead of spending halfheartedly, you make keen moves—boss moves. Children and even animals act instinctively, but as we grow, we mature, utilize the knowledge, and make logical decisions. We're adults, right? We are too grown not to have a budget. #toogrown

Now before we start, you're gonna mess this budget up for the first few months. You might even have a hiccup when you've been on it for a while too, but that's okay; stay the course. When I get too relaxed (swiping), not looking at my budget, that's when I mess up and get back to the basics.

The first step in the budget is to come up with your goals. Yep, that's right, back up to Chapter II and find *you some purpose* because you definitely won't get anywhere without targeting your success. Go on now! *And don't come back in this house until you're ready to stay and do some work.* (Some of y'all will get that.)

Write: What do you want to do with your money?

What kind of lifestyle do you want to have now? What lifestyle do you want to have in your future years?

What will you sacrifice to get the financial lifestyle you want for now and your future?

What needs do you want to take care of?

What dreams do you have that will cost money? Your wants are a vital part of your financial lifestyle, and they, too, can be added to the budget.

Goals

____

____

____

____

____

____

____

____

Write down your dreams and goals! Specifically, what do you want to accomplish? By when? How will you know when you meet the goal? Is this goal reasonable within the allotted time f rame you have given yourself?

Your next step is to analyze all of your money.

1. How much money do you have coming in after taxes from all sources?

TYPE OF INCOME	MONTHLY AMOUNT
Monthly Salary (take home pay)	
Side Hustle	
Child Support, alimony	
Bonuses/Commissions	
Rental Income	
Interest/Dividends	
Social Security, Pensions	

List all sources of income.

2. What expenses do you currently have? List every expense, even the corner store runs on your lunch break. Use your bank statements to help you.

EXPENSES	MONTHLY AMOUNT
Mortgage or rent	
Classroom expenses	
Dating	
Entertainment	
Credit Card payments	
Gas	
Internet & Cable	
Cell phone	
Vet	
Lawn service	

Write down all expenses (even your pets, tolls, investment accounts, lunch, etc.).

3. Analyze if you are in the red zone (overspending—you don't have enough income to cover your expenses) or the green zone (you have enough income to pay all of your bills and creditors. If you're in the red zone, it's time to get serious about your budget.
4. Figure out the money you have saved up for emergencies and retirement accounts. What's invested? Here's a good time to see what your net-worth is by calculating **all** assets minus debts.
5. Calculate all of your living expenses (revolving bills), debts, and the due dates.
6. Separately, you need to record when and how much is due to each creditor or bill so you can pay on time.

Now, it's time to set some tough parameters:

7. Here's where the tough part comes in: Sacrifice. Boundaries Activated! (I imagine *Power Rangers* saying that with their quick moves! Lol! Just go with it!) It's time to set some limits. Time to put your foot down. Time to speak up. Time to implement and enforce your boundaries! If you're in the red zone, something has to give, as in, you have got to give up some stuff—either your wants or your time.
   a) **Wants**: The items you don't need, like cable TV, eating out several times a week, buying extravagant gifts, subscriptions you don't use, elaborate vacations, parties, hanging out with people who influence your spending, etc. You gotta cut it out. Just say no!
   b) **Time**: If your bills are all relevant and necessary, you might need to invest some time into calling in and lowering your bills or adding another stream of income (i.e., side hustle or your own business, a part-time job, e-commerce opportunities, even a good network marketing business.). No matter what you're going to invest time.

8. Last but not least, allocate a dollar amount to every expense category. Leave no topic unturned, like healthcare, debts you owe to family members or friends, shopping, food, gas, insurance (this is a must), pet food, pet healthcare, beauty needs, etc.

What should you do if you find yourself upside down? Meaning you don't have enough money coming in.

If you're like me, you may find that you're in the red zone at the beginning and don't have enough money to take care of everything. If this is the case, you have a cash flow problem. You don't have enough cash flow to keep your house running properly. In order to increase your cash flow, you need to look at:

1. Cutting expenses (subscriptions, eating out, shopping, cable bill, trips, beauty treatments, etc.).
2. Getting an additional job or begin making money from your skills (your side hustle or business).
3. Making sure you are paying the correct amount of taxes by looking at your W-4. If you're getting money back from the IRS on a yearly basis, you're missing out on several hundred dollars a month that could be allocated toward your debt (go back to the previous section *Minimizing your Taxes)*. Again: Stop overpaying in taxes.

Overall, a budget is not going to suck the marrow from your bones. It's a strategic plan to tell your money where to go. But it takes hard work initially. Don't expect to master your budget in a speed of light. One person I helped took about five months to get it right. Make sure to make a new budget each month as things change, and don't deliberately sabotage by going over budget. I love how Hebrews 12:11 says it, "No discipline seems pleasant at the time, but painful. Later on, however, it produces a harvest..." It takes time, but eventually you'll find your groove along with the right budget sheet which is in harmony with your personality.

Monthly BUDGET PLAN

	Monthly take home pay (from all sources)		$______________	
Expense	**Amount**	**Budgeted**	**Spent**	**What's Left**
House				
Mortage/Rent				
Repairs				
Savings				
Emergency Fund				
Sinking Fund (Trip to Madagascar)				
Food				
Eating Out				
Groceries				
Utilities				
Electricity				
Phone				
Internet				
Debts				
Car Payment				
Student Loan #1				
Student Loan #2				
Credit Card				
Personal				
Dating				
Entertainment				
Clothes				
Hygiene				

Sample budget sheet (preview)

Go to bonus.findyourspark.info to download your free budget and goal sheets.

A budget can help you take down your debts. If you have debt, eliminating it should be your ultimate goal for the moment, and that's the vantage point of this book. Know that money is ***the*** top cause of stress (American Psychology Association), and many people refuse to deal with their money issues. People commit suicide over money (don't take this casually), give up their kids to give them a better life, allow crimes, commit crimes, divorce over financial issues, and get depressed over money problems because they see no way out. I'm here to tell you that it's possible. You CAN do this! The Most High doesn't want debt for you!

Creating your goals for your budget will help you concentrate on your *why*. Our goal with the budget is to account for every dollar and allocate it. Now, if that stresses you, as it does me, know that your budget can have designated categories for spending like *pocket money* or *incidentals*. For instance, I have a lump sum for my groceries, gas, eating out, and whatever I want in one category because it would stress me out if I had to budget that part of my life harshly. I still know what I can and cannot spend since I have allotted specific funds for these items. Because I drive minimally, gas is not a huge cost for me. I might want a bag of chips, a book, baking supplies, or to eat out, go to a movie, or accept an invite—it's what singles do! This category gives me peace of mind because all my other categories are scripted with precision. It's actually a lump sum that I leave in my account knowing all other tasks have been paid.

What's vital is that I *actually* follow the budget! Some people will argue against that because I don't have a gas category or groceries, etc. I still balance my budget down to 0.00. It works; it's how I paid off about $15K in debt within my first twelve months of starting this journey. I do what's going to get results for me and less stress. I know where I spend too much money. It's always in the same category. I tell you this, so you can script the budget that works best for you. Seriously, the only budget that matters is the one you follow and helps you CRUSH your goals (mic drop)! If you want to go fast the budget will conform. If you want to go slow because you can't give up something, well that's up to you. Your choices will show how bad you want to get out of debt or get to your goals.

How do you keep track? First, make sure you write down your budget on paper! Yes, you can still use a digital version, but there's something about a written budget that works. That's where I started every time I began eliminating debt.

Then I moved to an online spreadsheet. I like the digital version, but I always write down my goals and budget items on paper first. I used to hang up my schedule to pay items off and cross them off as I go! It's amazing! You can use digital apps as well, and you can find those in the bonus materials on my website at bonus.findyourspark.info. I use an excel spreadsheet because I like to plan my budget out by a year to see the entire vision (it keeps me motivated). It's still month by month, and I revisit it at least twice a month, even weekly if needed to make sure I'm staying on track. But I can see it easily from my phone and my computer. Having eyes on your budget is a great reinforcement! Trust me; if you're not looking at it, you're at the edge of the cliff with your spending. You can't make it and then never look at it. It's a living, breathing document.

How do I make sure I'm spending within my budget? Some people use envelopes or the cash method to put their funds in each category, which is excellent. Simply get an envelope for each category, put the money in there, and stuff it in your wallet, so you have what you planned to spend. If you set $50 for hair or nails, you'll put that in your grooming category.

However, I'm a digital girl, and I loathe carrying around cash because I lose it (I can't get cash back if I lose it). Envelopes are a *no* for me. I love swiping my card. If the thought of carrying around money frightens you, then keep track of your spending digitally.

1	-	Bill Collector	March 2021	April 2021	May 2021	June 2021	July 2021	August 2021	September 2021	October 2021
2										
3	Installment Debt	CREDIT CARD	$0.00	$0.00	$0.00	$0.00	$0.00	$0.00	$0.00	$0.00
4		MORTGAGE	-$1,351.61	-$1,351.61	-$1,351.61	-$1,351.61	-$1,351.61	-$1,351.61	-$1,351.61	-$1,351.61
5		TIMESHARE – UGH	$0.00	$0.00	$0.00	$0.00	$0.00	$0.00	$0.00	$0.00
6		CREDIT CARD CONSOLIDATIC	-$535.67	-$535.67	-$535.67	-$535.67	-$535.67	-$535.67	-$535.67	[redacted]
7		STUDENT LOAN	-$97.00	-$97.00	-$97.00	-$97.00	-$97.00	-$97.00	-$97.00	-$97.00
8		STUDENT LOAN	$0.00	$0.00	$0.00	$0.00	$0.00	$0.00	$0.00	-$300.00

Partial view of my digital budget. I can see monthly and yearly .

I have a note inside my phone for each pay period that shows me what I need to pay. As soon as I get my paycheck, I go down the list and check each one off (see the example in Chapter V: Get Organized). I have some items that come out automatically (especially my savings/ emergency funds) because they are a set amount. For fluctuating accounts, I pay each by hand every month. Then I hit the checkmark button on my list. I do not wait to pay any debts. If I budgeted to pay $200 more than the balance due, I make sure I pay it upfront! If you try to put your overhead on the back end, you WILL use this money, and it won't get you closer to your goals. I promise. Wherever you allocated the money, spend it there, and pronto! You're trying to create good habits, and to do so, you must follow through. Even though I don't use cash, I know exactly what I'm spending. Another tip is to write down how much you spend as you spend it. Sometimes you may have money left over in a category. If you get paid the same amount each paycheck, every month, then allocate those funds to a designated area like your emergency fund or debt (even if it's a dollar). You may even allocate it towards giving to others–a great reason for me to have some pocket money to give to the less fortunate.

What happens when life happens? What if you mess up on the budget? Congratulations and welcome! It happens. Just adjust it and keep going. Sometimes, you have to change the budget. An emergency will hit you and throw your budget off . Especially in the beginning, when you're still trying to establish your emergency fund. Will you take advantage of an opportunity? Possibly, but not without looking at your budget first and avoiding emotional spending. What makes budgets difficult is our persuasive environments and our lack of consistency. You have to be patient. A little sacrifice now will only build character and deeper pockets. You may have to pass on some opportunities and luxuries to remember why you started. It CAN wait!

Commit to a budget so you can succeed—give it the attention it needs. You have to put some skin in the game to see the results. Some of us wade through this task with ardor and grace, while others struggle. If the thought of creating a budget scares you, get a financial coach or CFP (Certified Financial Planner) for three to six months to help you develop your skills. Experts, financial tools, and financial memberships will also help you create your budget and give you a path for eliminating debt. It's a worthy investment to get an expert. You choose an expert in all the other areas of your life. You could do it yourself, but you know the expert is going to:

1. Save you time.
2. Direct you to helpful resources.
3. Eliminate the guessing.
4. Help you eliminate mistakes.

At one point, I used a combination of my own budgeting tool in excel, digital budgeting tools from popular sites, investing in a membership with financial experts (taxes, credit, debt, and wealth-building), and networking with others to learn. We all have different levels of what we need to do to flourish on our financial paths.

Overall, creating a budget can be a tedious process, but you don't have to go at it alone. You can have others help you and join in on your success. Serious couples and partners need to be on the same page when it comes to their money. You can't have one person budgeting and the other spending. It won't work. If you're single, find a budget buddy or accountability partner. You need someone you can discuss your budget with (if possible), and that will *check you* when needed. Who's the financial guru in your life? Find that person, have that conversation, and begin.

If you want financial success, create a budget and tell your money where to go. One place people have a hard time telling their money where to go is their emergency fund. Let's find out how this one crucial area can make or break your budget.

Hold Firm to the Emergency Fund

How many times do you want to start over with your finances? How much energy do you have built up that will allow you to continue falling down and getting back up? At some point, you'll be like me and say, *I was meant for more: life can't only be about working, paying bills, living paycheck to paycheck, and then dying.*" This life—your life—was meant for more!

To get more, we mustn't let the reality of life get in the way of crushing our goals. Your emergency fund is like the safety to your defensive line, you. And for your team to win, you need to have your emergency fund, a key player blocking whatever life throws at you. While your money is out there on offense, running plays to crush debt, and scoring major points in the investment world, your emergency fund will be your #1 safety net to life, putting a dent in your plan. Think offensive tackle.

We never know when an emergency will occur nor how much it will cost us. Let your emergency fund brace your fall ***when*** emergencies happen. Before you raise your finger, I know there are some life circumstances that you can never prepare for, but then again, that's why we have car, health, house, and life insurance policies, right? Your budget is not protected without an emergency fund.

Journal Entry, November 23, 2007

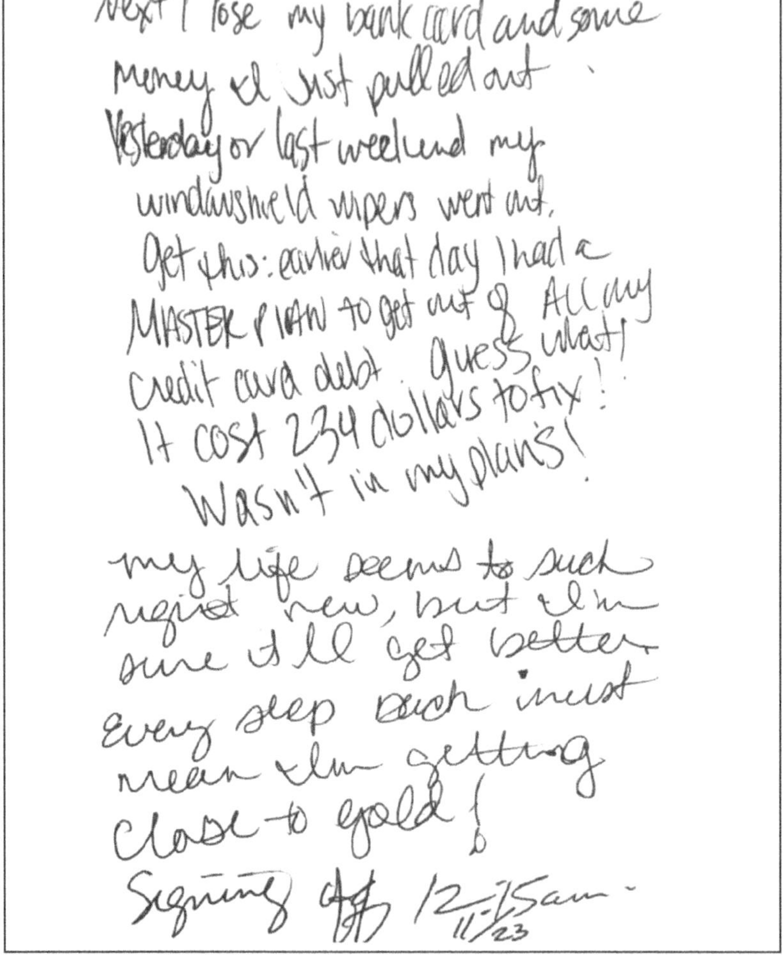

Next I lose my bank card and some
money I just pulled out
Yesterday or last weekend my
windshield wipers went out.
Get this: earlier that day I had a
MASTER PLAN to get out of ALL my
credit card debt. Guess what!
It cost 234 dollars to fix!
Wasn't in my plans!

my life seems to such
regret now, but I'm
sure it'll get better.
Every step each must
mean I'm getting
close to goal!
Signing off 12:15am
11/23

(I chuckle when I read about my younger self. Such passion! However, a plan without an emergency fund is fragile. An emergency fund remained a mystery well into my thirties.)

The very first goal in your budget is to **hold firm** and establish an emergency fund. Hold firm to the idea that this strategy is a winning play in your overall plans. Before you pay off your creditors, **pay yourself first**! Your creditors want their money, but they will be okay. They have the government's backing to bail them out during hard times, but who will bail you out? You have to make sure your household is protected first and foremost (food, shelter, water, clothing, utilities). If you despise asking for a handout or asking for help from family and friends, I implore you to create an emergency fund. At the same time, remember *a closed mouth doesn't get fed*, so ask for what you need if you find yourself in a dire situation while trying to get financially grounded (don't wear out your welcome). Your emergency fund will help you remain on track with your budget and save you from awkward moments or constantly asking for handouts.

The Pandemic of 2020 taught us that our jobs aren't as solid as we think. Companies had to lay off hard-working and loyal employees. And some of those same companies adopted models that help them run their businesses using fewer employees, teaching us that we can't solely depend on our jobs as our only source of income. It also opened our eyes that we (as individuals and a nation) operate with too much debt.

Think: Most people were bled dry in a matter of three to six weeks! Imagine if there had been no relief. What would've happened? Exactly why we need a form of self-banking, so we aren't scrambling when things around us are chaotic. When hard times come, you need to be able to grab from *your* stash.

Your emergency fund needs to consist of your savings, but it should also include such things as a living will, a will, auto, health and life insurance, and funeral plans. You need directives and funds in case something should happen to you. Someone should know where your money will go, who will take care of your loved ones, who has control over your medical and financial information, how your assets should be divided, and your final thoughts and procedures on what should happen if you are debilitated or die. We cannot pretend as if such things will never happen. To do so is living in a fairytale. Settle your mind and settle the minds of your loved ones by establishing your emergency fund and all that it should encompass. What is the minimum amount needed to be covered when difficulties come your way?

Remember, the goal is to have an emergency fund to help you prepare for future problems, which can happen the next moment or the next day. In fact, here's a prime a scenario of someone going back into debt no sooner than they got out because of a unique set of circumstances:

Person A has been debt-free before the Pandemic of 2020. But soon after, they were $30,000 in debt because of an emergency and shopping while stuck at home. They have a steady job, but not able to save much since becoming full time caregiver of their elderly father.

Person a wants to buy a house and invest in a business, but now the debt my cause issues. Should Person A pay off the debt first or save for a down payment? Should they start a business to increase their cash flow?

Do you see anything we discussed prior (emotional spending, crises, etc.)? You might be asking how they could allow themselves to get back into debt so quickly. Didn't they learn their lesson the first time? Why don't they have emergency funds to pay for such costs as healthcare? Life can turn around quickly. And who's been preparing for a pandemic all their life, right! So many questions and thoughts to address, but the elephant in the room is: What exactly should they do? I'll let you decide. Discuss it with your circle, but remember to be gracious. We all operate with what we think is best at the time. There are many paths to the same solution. What would you do?

I have had several of these conversations with people asking a similar question regarding house buying: debt or down payment? What is most important? That's a question each person, each couple has to decide. I know my answer. However, I must abide by the will of my client's goals. Each decision must be their own, and something they must live with, without regrets (*hopefully*). Simultaneously, I must hold each person to those goals, educate, and help my clients see the bigger picture (sometimes that challenging them and giving them a new perspective).

In this example, this is why you establish the emergency fund: to avoid going back into debt. Because you may be just starting, you need to make a goal. How much should you put in your quick emergency fund? I'd think about the totality of your household. On average, how much do emergencies cost you? As a homeowner, that differs for me, but generally, I want a minimum of $3,500 in my quick emergency fund or enough to cover my deductibles–house, auto, health. My next goal would be to have at least one month's worth of expenses in my fund. If you take care of others in your household, you might want to set aside a specific amount, like $500-$1,000 per person. Some people are okay with a $1,000 emergency fund (starting out). I would've been scrambling if I had only set that amount aside. When kids bring home viruses, you get sick and have to miss work, or your car breaks down is a recipe for disaster if you don't have funds to combat such issues. Emergencies can wipe out your money quickly. So, do what's best for your situation, starting with a minimum of $500 to $1,000. Tuck it away in another account that's not as easily accessible to spend and earns higher returns than a regular checking account.

As I wrote this book and on my journey to paying off debts, my precious fur baby Angel passed away. The next day the A/C stopped working, the same week the bathroom needed repairs, two weeks later the garage door broke down, and maybe six to eight weeks later, the check engine light came on in my car, then it stopped running, and then it became trial and error! After fixing some minor issues with my car, I had a costly problem with my house and my car. Had I not had an emergency fund or a budget, I would've been all over the place, and my budget and the debt-free plan would be toast. The old me would've only had credit cards only to pay for the emergencies (consider that some emergencies are cash only). Thankfully, I was able to continue on my plan because I'd put about $3,500 in my quick emergency fund before the pandemic hit—what a brutal year. I had to use it, move some budgeting items around, and eventually add more. **Note:** Don't be bummed out to use your emergency funds! That's why it's there. Just rebuild it, and keep going, pressing pause on some goals. What's the amount that you want in your first emergency fund?

Over one year, during the pandemic, I spent almost $11,000 on emergencies. I'm grateful I could pay it without adding more debt, but I had to focus on rebuilding my fund. Therefore, I urge you to **pay yourself first** and thank yourself later. Pay the minimums on the debt until you establish a quick emergency fund—this is a smaller amount to put out the minor nuisances we encounter.

I hope you see that living life on the edge (without emergency funds) will give you an over-the-cliff experience every time problems arise. Instead, put the proper plans in place, and you and your loved ones will reap the benefits. Your emergency doesn't replace your views or trust in God; it simply helps you manage the resources God has given you. A household without an emergency fund is like building a house on sand.

Fill YOUR Pockets

Even when you are itching to give your money to the creditors first, don't! Fill your own pockets by paying yourself first and setting yourself up for success. This step is so crucial to a successful financial journey that if you fail to do so, you will be participating in an epidemic rat race starring, directed by, and executively produced by YOU. Remember, by **minimizing your taxes**, you have already begun the process of filling your pockets—no more free loans to the government. Then, you can use this money to support your newfound habit of **paying yourself first** by financing your emergency fund! To get more money to increase your cash flow and fund your goals try some of the following.

1. Cancel subscriptions.
2. Avoid late fees by not overspending and paying on time.
3. Find coupons and discounts. (Couponing in itself can help you start a side hustle.)
4. Call and lower your bills. That means you must get on the phone and call your providers—all of them —to lower your bills. Yes, CALL THEM! Ask for deals you would get as a new customer, go to the basic plan, see what work or partnership discounts they may provide.
5. Stop eating out or drastically lower how often you do.
6. Start making money from your skills.
7. Get a part-time job.
8. Start a home-based business.
9. Sell items you own (your overflow items and not ones that are dear to you).
10. Stop handing out money that you don't have. The first place to start increasing your cash flow is by saving more of your money in the first place (less gifting, lending money, paying for miscellaneous items at work, etc.).

11. Correct and update your W-4 with a tax expert.
12. Write a book.
13. Be an affiliate marketer.
14. Make and sell digital products.

Among many who are wealthy, there is an unwritten rule, "everything is negotiable." You'd think the people who *have* money to overpay would pay the price. Um, no. They negotiate, and you can too. I learned this from someone I dated and by watching people who have money. One person negotiated *everything* (it felt that way). I noticed, "ask, and then ask again"— that's in the playbook. Be firm. Be prepared to walk away or cancel (don't show desperation). If you're negotiating one-on-one, try to come up with a win-win scenario.

So, what if *they* say no; there's no harm done. Get used to hearing *no* so often that you don't flinch because, in order for you to get some deals and lower your bills from service providers or negotiate that car price, you need confidence and determination. Your goal is to reduce your bills, lower interest rates, cancel subscriptions, and even shop around for insurance—use a broker. Be prepared to walk away from unnecessary expenses that do not suit you. Most of the items we have, we don't need. And right now, if you're struggling, your cash flow is what is going to get you to next week and next month. The less you have going out, the more you have in your pocket. So look for ways to pay less.

Keep your utilities and other necessities turned on, but you don't need cable TV, a music subscription, gym subscription, several streaming services, hair services every week, etc. Figure out what you can live with and what you can live without, including what you can do yourself and what you need others to do for you.

At one point, I had a *rinky-dink* phone that held a few pictures but could call and get some text messages. My signifi cant other at the time was like, “When are you going to get a real phone?” Listen, touch screen phones were out by then, and my phone was not one of them. It had gel buttons and felt hollow. That phone could call, text, and fit in the small pocket of your pants. Baaaby! I do not play. I will be super cheap to get to my goals! Y’all better ask somebody! Ramen noodles, .99¢ tacos, grilled cheese, and receipts that have coupon codes for a free burger were and still are in my playbook! I am the same person who told my family that I would stop giving gifts (except for kids), and that I was no longer accepting them, either. I made it my standard to do experi-ences together and enjoy other people’s company. Besides, gifts don’t satisfy my soul, especially when you’re single, and you can buy (or finance —eyes rolling) yourself whatever you desire. Whether bills or my habits, I make the necessary cuts to fill my pockets.

Here’s the jig: Sacrifice now and live wealthier later, or you can continue to play around now, living paycheck to paycheck and panic later. What I'm saying is unpopular. I'm telling you to be patient. I'm asking you to unsubscribe to the *fast paced, fix it now*, magic button syndrome, so you can develop the character of someone who *can* welcome wealth. What are you deciding?

Level the Debt

The three credit bureaus have people wrapped so tightly around credit scores it’s ridiculous. People are more focused on the score than the actual debt; ain't that a trip! At times, it seems as though the companies you owe decide your fate when it comes to credit. Your scores can deny you access to key features that fuel your lifestyle, such as finding a job (yes, they are pulling your credit nowadays), how much you pay for your car, insurance, residence and its location, whether you must put a deposit on your cable, phone, or utility bills, and who knows what's next.

You pay a higher rate for items when you don't have good credit. That means your interest rates are higher, and instead of catching a break (like rich people or people who have good credit), you get penalized at EVERY STEP of the way, making it even harder to live life. Poor credit costs you thousands of dollars, keeping you in debt and from financial freedom. People with good credit enjoy life at a cheaper cost. And those who don't worry about credit (because they only pay cash or leverage it in a way most don't), well, they are ahead of the game–because it is a game.

Consider this: Two people can buy the same car at the same dealership, and one pays a significantly higher amount for the vehicle while the other pays several thousand dollars less because of the differences in their credit scores.

Now historically, we've seen unequal costs of goods due to systematic racial inequalities in America. Whether it's still happening or not is another discussion. But now, credit and credit scores affect us all. Take this example below: If you have great credit, you will pay significantly less in interest than someone who has poor credit. How many times do you want to pay for things? $18K in interest is another car within itself! Again, how much more do you want to pay for items than your counterparts?

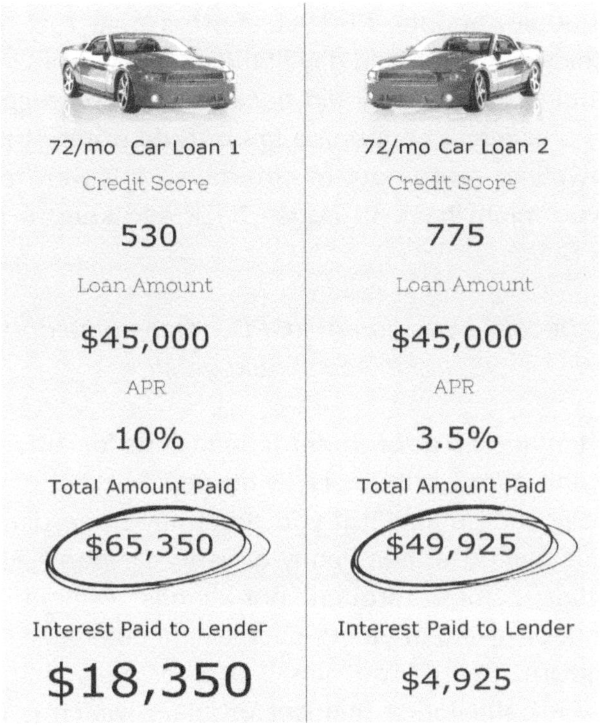

This example is provided for information purposes only.

The car note for Car Loan 1 would approximately be $835 versus roughly $695. Because I'm cheap and have never liked car payments, it's a whole "NO!" to both options! But for someone whose income is sufficient may have no problem with such costs. However, we have to get out of the mind frame of being okay with *just making the payment.* Being able to afford the price could have you paying for two cars, but you only get to drive off the lot with one. I asked a group of people on social media if they could get a house at a 550 credit score, would they?

Now I'm asking you, would you?

Most people said yes, and a few asked about the interest rates. People, people, PEOPLE: 550 is near rock bottom! The bank will have a field day (if they even allow it) ravaging and robbing you as they did back during the irresponsible lending practices of subprime loans. **Side note**: At the time of this writing, rent is out of control, so if it were possible heck, you might have to house hack and keep it rolling... (shoot)! But...

"Just because you can AFFORD it at the time does not mean you should get it!"

We have made up ***debtrimental*** definitions for "afford". You really can't afford it if you're living paycheck to paycheck. You really can't afford it if you don't have one dime to fix problems that arise. See, many of us try to spend every last dime that comes through our hands without saving, investing, or giving anything back to the community. A 550 credit score means you have an error, very little credit, possibly a behavior or mindset problem (which is fixable). The only issues that are fixable are the ones you face. If you plan on repairing the dilemma, target it. If not, avoid it, but it's still going to be your issue. That doesn't necessarily mean you did it on purpose or that you directly caused the bad credit. It just means that there's a problem to be fixed, so get to it.

Stay with me. Let's take a breath...

Namaste...And breakdown the overall mechanics of credit.

Credit determines how well you can juggle borrowed money–debt.

So that means that you NEED DEBT to build credit. Put yourself in the middle of the picture, juggling all your debts. Why are we happy with all of this debt?

I don't want to count people's pockets, but we congratulate each other on debts we buy all the time. And then we give glory to God for all these items we've charged under our names. Was it really God or your impatience? Was it God or your adoption of what the world says you should have? We take uncalculated risks every day when we add on insurmountable debts without a plan to pay them off, meanwhile investments are "scams". Then we add God into the mix as if that gives Him glory. We need to be careful when we take such approaches. If God is getting zero glory...okay you get the point. I will say this: If we put God first in all things, then we might find ourselves on the other side of debt, displaying good stewardship, something for us all to mull over.

And what can be said about a country that wants its citizens overloaded with debt? As we move on, I *really* want you to assess the impact of your debt and how credit takes a front-row seat.

The Basics

Creditors decide (based on your score) how much of a risk you are before they go into business with you. Low scores below 670 are fair to poor, and scores ranging from 670-850 are good to excellent.

How long do you want to manage debt? Because to keep up with your credit, you have to have debt or the appearance of debt (secured cards and loans). Debt keeps you busy, keeps you failing, and keeps you from living a life worth living.

Sure, you're happy now, of course, but the decision to stay in debt will show its ugly side sooner or later.

Tip: If you do not have credit, don't apply to get a load of credit cards. Did you know there are religious groups who refuse to live with debt nor accept usury? It's possible. Harder, but possible. Your creditworthiness can be proven with the proper documents (rent, utilities, bills, etc.), but it takes patience (and cash) to get what you want without credit—keyword: patience. Yes, getting a credit card is an easy way, but there are other options to build credit for young credit novices, especially if you're being careful to avoid debt.

"Don't let the world tell you how to live your life. You don't have to adopt or subscribe to every trend or new sensation that the world advertises."

Now, I'm going to be a bit contentious here: There are two sides to the coin when you think of credit. Some people will vouch for using credit, and some say never use credit! Some people leverage it for rewards or self-paying assets like real estate. Just remember: It is all debt.

By the way, don't fall into the hype about there being good debt and bad debt. All debt has a negative connotation. I don't care if you're leveraging it. Don't get it twisted, and *always* have an exit plan when life presents you with no viable options other than debt. When creditors are calling you to collect, it's not a friendly and easy conversation. When you get letters in the mail, pink slips, and threats to take your property or seize your paycheck, there is nothing good about those situations. I don't care if you are paying for education or a house; it's debt! Are we clear?

Again, always have an exit strategy when signing up for a loan, credit, or other debt.

Some people use credit cards to get the rewards and pay them off each month. These people use their credit card like their debit card, and it gets paid off every time they use it. Most of the people I know who use this technique were taught this very early in life, and they don't accrue debt on their credit cards. They manage their money very well. I, too, have used this method, which helps to avoid paying interest each month. The rewards are not life-changing, but I do call it a win-win when I can get dollars back for spending money I will spend anyway (i.e., rent, groceries, etc.).

If you're tempted (of course, you'll be tempted) to go back into a lifestyle of debt, I would highly advise against using credit. Don't do it at all while you're weak because you're trying to change habits, especially if you're addicted to the *swish* of the *swipe*. And if you have a low credit score due to your spending habits and poor money management, I'd avoid trying to juggle such systems. Focus on rebranding your money mindset and developing routines that build success. Don't tempt yourself with credit cards or personal loans. Put the cards down, take them out of your purse or wallet, and step away! Before I even knew about strategies, I did this. I simply stashed my cards somewhere to give myself zero opportunity to use them while I got myself out of trouble. In my mind, they were going to be paid off and never utilized.

However, it didn't quite happen like that. I ran the cards back up, and started the process all over again. That's the debt cycle you need to avoid.

Now because I'm a recovering people pleaser, I don't like giving ultimatums, but I'm going to be definitive about this one key area:

If you're trying to get out of debt and have a toxic relationship with credit cards, leave the credit cards, loans, secured credit cards, and anything else that leads you to more debt alone. Just stop. You cannot fix your situation with the same mindset, the same habits, the same attitude, the same skills that got you there in the first place.

We know credit plays a vital role in our society. Again, sometimes we are so focused on the credit score that we don't look at the debt. We've been programmed.

I see so many people full of credit rooms and conversations trying to improve their credit scores. If people would first focus on getting rid of their debt, they wouldn't be worried about their credit scores! I paid off a credit card, and my score jumped 30 points, and then added something back on and it decreased about 30 points. You can fix the score! But the debt will still be there if you don't pay (avoid court letters).

That car can wait. That house can wait. Whatever it is can wait. We try to do things on our time, the world's time, in a flash, and outdo God's time frame for our lives. Slow down. Because the reality is that removing items off your report does not necessarily remove the responsibility that you *still* owe money to your creditor. Come on, my fellow Believers: *Give to Caesar what is his!*

> ***Note****: there are incidents where the company sells your debt to a collection agency because they count it as a loss for accounting purposes. The debt collection company now owns the debt, in which they paid very little. Since you don't have a signed agreement with the debt collection company, you can argue that you don't owe the said company. But the law allows the collection agencies to report the debt on your credit report for up to seven years. The reporting time could change depending on your communication with and commitment to the collection agency. Your responsibility to pay the debt can be challenging when the original company will no longer take the payment, and the new company is trying to get several hundred dollars from you, knowing they paid (as an example) fifty bucks. Hmph!*

The purpose of fixing your credit is so that you can level the debt to zero while simultaneously filling your pockets with more money. As you pay down debt, your credit score goes up, and as your credit score goes up, you can renegotiate your mortgage loans, your car loans, your credit cards (look for 0.00% balance transfers and 0% interest for several months), and so on, giving you access to more cash flow. That could save you hundreds or thousands of dollars in yearly interest. The more cash flow you have available, the faster you can pay down your debt.

For most people, getting to a place where they are comfortable and believing that they don't need credit takes time & money (the idea *will* continue to fluctuate). My goal is not to **depend** on credit, but be able to leverage it (on the business side of things.) Until then, here are some steps to help you restore your credit.

Credit repair is different for everyone, but there are key items that you can do to repair your credit. Anyone can fix their credit. And at the same token, they can also hire professionals to do it for them. There's nothing wrong with either strategy. Make sure you establish the time and follow through if you're going to do it yourself. And if you're hiring someone, make sure they educate you during the process. It does nothing to fix your credit and then recycle the same habits which put you in the same position months or years later. While specialist are working on your behalf, gain some knowledge to help your credit stay in an excellent position.

Did you know that in Germany, they still mostly use cash? Credit cards are not widely used and are paid at the end of every month. Yeah, that's right! The bank will draft your account to pay off your credit card each month. And if you refuse to pay, they can take over your account until the money is paid back in full. Yikes! Now that's boss! They are not playing with anyone in Germany! Can we say, "*Give me my money?*" (clap when you do it for effect, lol) But you know what that means, right? They curve their citizens from having too much debt. If they can do it, why can't you? **How did I find this information?** I was having a financial conversation on social media with a lady from Germany. Imagine surrounding yourself with others, and you'll learn all kinds of great information. Now, if you're like me, you're heading straight to your favorite search engine.

Key tips to repairing your credit

Here is a guide to how your credit score is calculated. However, the exact algorithms reside in the hands of the **for profit** credit bureaus (Equifax, Experian, TransUnion), the three ***widely known*** companies responsible for collecting information about your financial habits. Debt collectors report your information to these bureaus, which results in your credit report. Sometimes that information is valid, and sometimes it's not (that's when you have to dispute).

Based on your Credit Report, you are given a credit score. There are many types of credit scores (i.e. auto, credit card, mortgage) created from different scoring models such as FICO (Fair Isaac Corporation) or Vantage scores. Your score tells lenders how well you are at borrowing money, a.k.a. managing debt. Different models show different scores because various components taken from your credit report are weighted differently. The following covers the features of the FICO scoring model.

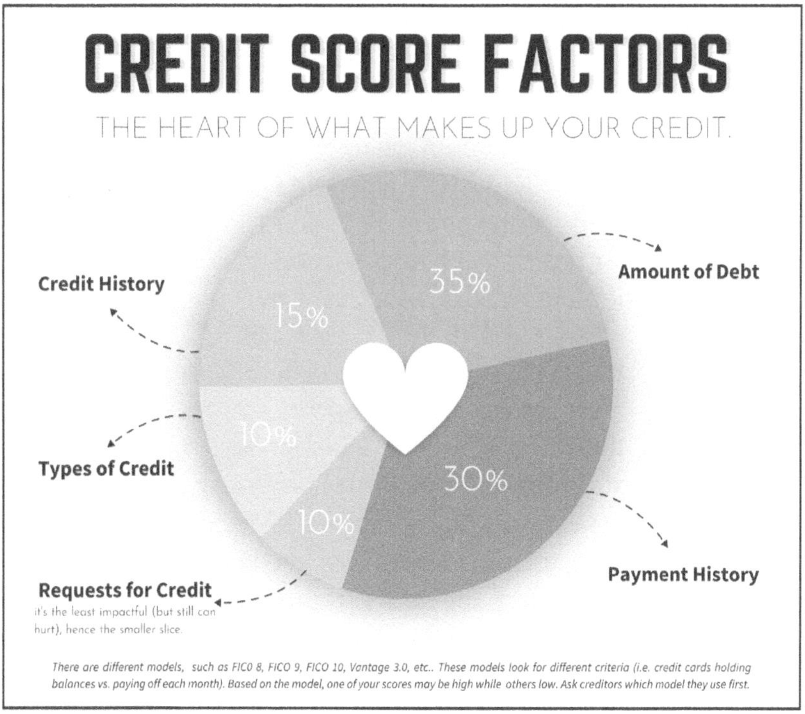

Credit Score Factor Explanations

Payment history: Keeps track of how you pay your bills (on time, late, missed payments, etc.) It is vital to pay on time. Late payments take you down quickly!

Amount of debt: The next big-ticket item tracks how much total debt you have. (This does not include owing your family and friends, by the way; pay them what you borrowed if gave your word to do so!) You can have a lot of debt and a great credit score and still be denied credit (i.e., personal loans and mortgage loans). Easy fix: Get rid of the debt. Some people say to keep a small amount on a credit card. I say just pay it off every month because it's one less thing to worry about. More than likely you have enough on your plate than to worry about small algorithms.

Credit history: This determines how long you've had credit. Think about the age of your credit accounts. The oldest accounts help your score. The purpose here is to see your historical pattern of borrowing money. As accounts age, they help your score.

Types of credit: This tells a lender the different types of credit you own, installment or revolving. Installment means that you'll eventually pay off the debt because you have set payments that will end. Revolving credit is never-ending as long as the account is open. You can charge, pay it off , and then charge again. It's cyclical.

Requests for credit: Inquiries are requests for credit. When companies run your credit report so you can obtain credit with them, it is reported as a *hard* inquiry or *soft* inquiry. **Hard inquiries** have the potential to lower your score if you have too many requests. These inquiries stay on your report for two years. When you are seeking to borrow money from creditors they will run your credit resulting in a hard inquiry. No more than two to three inquiries *is* reasonable within two years according to the bureaus. **Soft inquiries** do not harm your scores. These are inquiries that you request, and some companies can run these inquiries as well for you without damaging your score as they don't show up on your credit report.

Tips on Credit Rebuilding

1. Get a copy of your credit report from annual-creditreport.com for free (once a year) from each credit bureau. Analyze your reports to see what is on them. **Please note**: If you're reading this during the pandemic, citizens can get weekly updates on their credit reports.
2. Ensure the correct information is reporting accurately, such as dates, addresses, public records, accounts, balances, late payments, charge offs, liens, bankruptcy, repossessions, evictions, inquiries, etc.
3. Dispute. If anything is inaccurate, you want to dispute that information. There's a process for disputing that requires you to write a letter to the credit bureau explaining why you're contesting the information. You should send two forms of identification, get it notarized, and send it certified mail. (You see why people hire someone to do this?) You must be patient when disputing. You can easily search for sample letters online or download a few resources at bonus.findyourspark.info. Make sure you make the letters unique to you.
4. When writing your letters get to the point. A sob story is not going to convince the bureaus to remove items from your report. Challenge what needs to be challenged using the law and any evidence that you have. And under no circumstances should you reveal or acknowledge that the debt is yours. That's their job to verify, not yours. Keep it simple.
5. What should you dispute? You can dispute anything, but you should dispute inaccurate information and information you want to verify: the wrong balance, inquiries you did not request, incorrect dates, addresses, accounts that are not yours, charge offs, etc., anything you deem is wrong. You can dispute

the validity of the account, even if the account is yours. Legally, your creditor must verify that the account is yours within a timely manner. Honestly, the disputing process can take a while, but it can also help you boost your scores if successful. Please note that it doesn't excuse you from paying what you owe, as some companies will try to sue you for the debt. Another caution: During your disputes, please note that creditors may update positive or negative information, which will cause your score to fluctuate. Be patient, and dispute ten items or less each time.

6. Make sure to dispute negative accounts that are most recent within the last two years. Other negative accounts could be helping your score because of their age, so if removed, they could cause your score to go down.
7. Disputing directly with your creditors, especially if the account is older, could restart your statute of limitations. Creditors are required to remove debts from your account after seven years, depending on the type of debt. Bankruptcies can last from 10-12 years. However, contacting and making agreements to pay can cause your debt to be on your report longer. Sometimes writing to the creditor for a pay-for-delete is best, where the creditor will erase your debt when you pay. I have done this with negative medical accounts. You must get this in writing and not by phone. If you do happen to get it by phone, you will have to track who you spoke with (ask for a manager) and track down the recording. You may have to call back numerous times if they fail to uphold the agreement. Save yourself time, make sure you get it in writing, and beware of the verbiage used. If it says *"It will satisfy a portion..."* nerp, no ma'am, no sir...next! Ensure that the wording is in your favor, and

if you don't understand, say, "I need help!" and ask for an explanation.

8. Never dispute online. Can you? Yes! But you give up part of your disputing rights when you do so, according to the Fair Credit Reporting Act. You don't *actually* read all those boxes and agreements you check, now do you? I didn't think so. Disputing online gives you a limited number of reasons to dispute; therefore, you don't always get to explain the exact reason why you're disputing. And once you dispute online, the obligation to delete your negative information becomes difficult because you gave up your rights. So, write or fax into your friendly credit bureau and wait patiently. If you don't have the patience, pay someone. Your time is valuable, and you should use it wisely. If you have the time and the patience, then get to writing those letters and make sure you keep all your records and originals, especially if you have to sue.
9. Do you want to see your scores skyrocket? Start paying down debt and fast! Choose your credit cards first. There's nothing like a good rise in your score when your credit utilization (the amount of credit you're using versus how much you have available to use) is under 30%, but even better when it's under 10%. When you're paying down credit cards, make sure you do more than the minimum payment amount. You cannot get to financial freedom paying the minimums, so budget how much you will overpay. Some gurus say pay two payments (weeks apart) on the debt each month as part of an algorithm to boost your score. Frankly, that's too much work to be worried about a score. Pay what you need to pay and keep it moving. Worry about crushing the debt; the score will come.

10. After credit cards, pay off your loans. Your personal loans are usually lower in interest, costing you less. And sometimes your credit profile needs a different type of credit reporting. When I moved a credit card balance (to avoid high interest) to a personal loan, I saw my score increase (your results may be different).
11. Make on-time payments—another way to boost your credit score. Paying on time not only keeps negative information off your credit, but you avoid paying late fees and extra processing fees to restart your service. How much have you paid in fees this year?
12. Avoid applying for too many accounts at any given time. One or two in a 12–24-month period is best. Creditors who want to do business with you don't want to see your credit report pulled too many times. You look desperate. For auto loans and mortgages, you get about 30 days to "shop." Because you're usually looking around to get the best deal, it's okay to get multiple inquiries for these specific purchases and avoid the negative hits a lot of inquiries can cause.
13. Tradelines. All of the accounts on your credit report are tradeline accounts—a line of credit. Another way to boost your score is to have a fiscally responsible family member or family friend add you to one of their in-good-standing credit lines. This will help to decrease your credit utilization because you can increase your credit availability. In addition, you can inherit their good payment history. But make sure the credit history does not outdate you (your date of birth). You can't have a forty-year credit history and are only twenty-five years old! Make sure, however, that their creditor will report to the bureaus. Though the law says you must have access to the account, would it hurt if you simply denied the card sent to you or destroyed it? I suggest you get super clear about having the card with your credit benefactor. Tradelines are a great way to help your kids learn

good credit skills as they step into the world as an adult. It works if you keep the cards in good standing with no late payments.

14. Last (not final), make sure you have a mix of credit between installment and revolving accounts. Remember: Installment accounts, like a car note, have an end date. Revolving accounts are continuous, like your credit cards, because you can recharge them at any time. A way to build up your credit mixture with protection is by getting a secured loan or credit card, where your money takes the role of how much you can charge. You're backing the loan, and in return, the creditor will report your on-time payments to the creditors. These can be tricky because you still have to make sure you don't spend too much money on the card, or your utilization will be too high, thus lowering your score. (See how tedious this can be?) Getting a rebuilder loan that is a certificate of deposit (CD) is an alternative way. Depending on the financial institution you choose, they company loans you the money for the CD and you pay it back in installments, or you establish the CD with your money and then borrow against thus paying it back in installments to be reported on your credit report. Your credit mixture will get a boost, and it will also help you with on-time payments. You can obtain various secured accounts. Some provide you with access to buy products (jewelry, gaming systems, TVs, etc.), and they work. I repeat put this same energy into paying off the debts and disputing inaccuracies on your report, your scores will be fine in time.

Tip: Go to bonus.findyourspark.info for additional tips about Credit Repair.

Disputing your credit gets you a better score; however, paying off our debts fast and with intensity will have a quicker impact on your credit scores. Because you have 100% control of credit utilization (which is 30% of your score), paying your debt directly impacts your scores. Plus, you'll generate more cash flow to continue to tackle your goals. As you begin to understand credit better, you will realize that it's not something you want to rest on for your personal finances forever (keyword: personal). The people I know roaming freely about the earth can do so in retirement because they are debt-free, not because of their credit score, but because of their behavior. It's a freeing experience.

Get to a place where credit is not normalized. Work hard to save and pay for things in cash. Credit is king in some worlds, and cash is king in others! If you can't pay for it, wait! The effort you put into denormalizing debt will make a difference in building wealth in your finances. Debt is incongruent to building wealth and becoming financially free. So, repair your credit if you have a low credit score, leverage it responsibly, and live debt-free. Don't let credit determine your value. And when you start getting tons of offers in the mail, throw them away. Stop being fazed by the credit offerings, and be strategic about how you use credit.

Persistence is the key to repairing your credit. If you have the gumption to do it yourself, go for it. On the other hand, if you want credit experts to do it for you, I'm here for it, too, because your time is a form of currency: it's your greatest asset. And hiring others to fix your credit buys back your time.

I'm all for leveraging credit, using the rewards, and getting good deals, but the goal for this book and for those us who have had a *debtrimental* relationship with credit have to first break this courtship with a better mindset and habits to follow. Tackle your debt like it's the enemy. The Bible says, "the borrow is a slave to the lender." And we know how we feel about slavery right?

I don't want people to just look good, but be good–on the inside. Get your glow back. Find Your Spark! I want us to be able to give bigger, following through with doctors orders because we have the money, walking our family across academic stages without debt.

The credit game is never-ending, and it's just one aspect of your overall Financial Journey.

Getting Rid of Debt

Without debt and creditors pressuring you, you're free to think, build, and conquer. Watch how your stress levels decrease when your decisions increase your cash flow.

While you fix your credit, focus on ways to pay off debt. If you want and need extra money, you could start a side hustle or business using your gifts, get a part-time job, utilize cash back apps, do contract work, tutor, babysit, donate create a digital product, take surveys, and so much more! Get creative, but use it to ditch the debt!

There are two ways most people choose to pay off debt: **Debt avalanche** versus **Debt snowball**. Either strategy will work. And at the end of the day, what matters is getting rid of your debt.

Debt avalanche: You pay the debt with the highest interest rate first and continue this same process continuously. Once you pay off this debt (while still paying minimums on other debts), you use that money toward the next debtor. With this strategy, you will pay the least amount of interest and win over creditors who would love to make the most off of you.

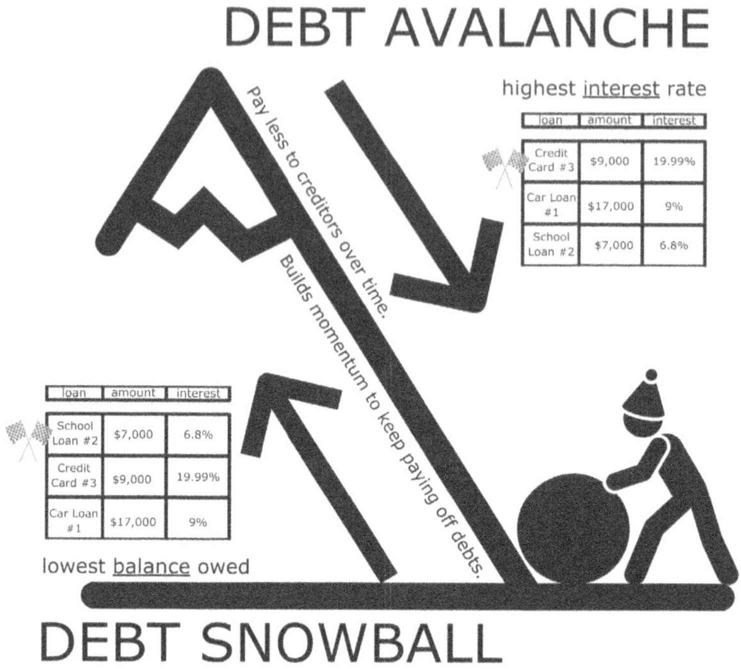

They say never pay more for anything than you have to (negotiate). Your largest debt may take a while to pay off on this plan, so be prepared to encourage yourself. If you have the stamina, go for it because numerically, it makes for solid financial cents.

Debt snowball: You pay off your debts from the least to the greatest amount, no matter the interest rate. Once you pay off one debt (while paying the minimums on all other debts), you move to the next debtor and use the money you were paying on the previous debt to add to your minimum payment on the next one. And you keep going until you are debt-free. When you understand the behavioral patterns of people, you will grasp that this method gives you a boost in morale and the willpower to keep going. Money is about your behavior. If you don't care about how much you pay in interest at the end of the finish line and want to make sure you keep the momentum going, this option is for you (the option I choose to use because I move to strike faster. I also take delight in crossing off the debt I post on my refrigerator door. It may even entice you to get a side hustle or extra job to get the job done faster once you see your success!

All in all, get out of debt so you can begin to create wealth.

Obtain Your Full Emergency Fund and Deeds

Once the extraneous debt is gone, you can now seek a full emergency fund, one in which your household can survive off for a minimum of six months. Some experts say three to six months; however, 2020 was brutal, and preparation is key. Had we been prepared with a decent emergency fund, many of us would've been more confident about our financial ability. I prefer six to twelve months (leaning more to twelve; however, choose the best option for you. Looking ahead, I feel we may need more than that if we hit a severe depression and the markets fall. The most crucial action is that you are operating with a strategic plan. No plan is full proof, but it's better to be armed than not--which do you prefer?

It can be tempting to go back to spending money lavishly, traveling, and buying everything you denied yourself—don't do it, or you'll be back in debt. Assign your money to go to your full emergency fund, paying off your house or paying toward a down payment and investment accounts. We don't just want to live for now; we want to think about the future. Remember, you can still have everything you want, but put it in the budget and pay cash or pay it off fast!

To establish a full emergency fund, calculate how much it costs to cover your monthly expenses and multiply that by the number of months you want to be saved up, at minimum, three months.

Use this easy equation below to establish how much you need in your emergency fund account:

____________ X	____________ =	____________.
1 month living expenses.	**# of months you want saved up.**	**Total needed in fund.**

Remember the money you were using to pay off your debt? Well, now you have a surplus of cash to fund your emergen-cies! Once you have paid off debts (except the mortgage), re-evaluate your budget to include the full emergency fund and map a plan to secure the deed to your mortgage(s). Now you're in a perfect place to rapidly put away money into your emergency fund and then pay off your mortgage.

Side note: Most people say a mortgage is good debt, but debt is just that: debt. If you look at how amortization on a house mortgage *truly* affects your mortgage payment, you will agree (see bonus materials). I know it's hard to get around this notion because we have normalized debt. We have normalized rapid results. We have normalized impatience. We have standardized the urgency of now. What happened to *saving until you could afford to buy* something? *Didn't she just say this?* Yes, I did! But we need to hear it again and again until we STOP normalizing debt!

Well, what about buying a house? A house is most times the biggest purchase we'll ever make (along with student loans, it seems these days). Most people cannot afford to pay for a house at the time of signing their contracts. ***Nonetheless,*** we should be putting ourselves in a position to make the best possible deal. One with a low interest rate, a plan to pay it off in record time, have a decent down payment and know all the other details about the home buying (PMI (private mortgage insurance), property taxes, interest rates vs. APR, types of loans-FHA or conventional, buying points, getting preapproved, etc.). I got into my house because I could afford the payment, and my Realtor convinced me that it was a more viable option than renting. I never wanted a home because of the tremendous responsibility—and it is! But now I have choices. I can sell and make a profit, borrow from myself to fund other investments, or become a landlord and add another income stream! (**Wayment**: it's not as easy as it comes off. There's work to be done with every decision.) I like the amenities that come with homeownership when you have lovely neighbors who want their community to thrive and create a safe and nurturing place for their children to grow up. I love having a secure place to park no matter what time I come home. I can provide respite to others needing a hand, and I don't have to give their name to the "front office; I get to decide. And there's the quietness (*depending on your neighbors*)—so many beautiful things.

Tip: If you're already in a house make sure your life insurance policy will cover the cost of your house, salary, and cost of living for those who are under your care in the event of your untimely death (even if you use the equity as an investment).

The beauty of owning real estate is that part of your money is going into the equity of the house, thus allowing you to sell and recoup what you have put into the house or more. And some people borrow against it to fund other investments. For the most part, it's not like watching coins fall through a net (unless it is steadily losing value), it's more like planting a seed, nurturing it, and watching it grow to its full potential.

The most common way people buy houses is to secure a loan from the bank, which is a form of debt. If you can buy your house with no debt, great! However, most of us are going to look at our options and take on the debt. And that's what's real, so buy it and make sure you either leverage your real estate and have an exit strategy—pay it oĀ in record time, rent it out, or sell at a higher price. Make sure you buy within your means because too much house can be no one's house if you miss several payments.

In review, obtain your full emergency fund, then get the deed to your house (whether you pay for it or renters, *okay!*) and continue on to welcoming wealth. In all honesty, if you've done that you're already ushering in wealth for you and your family. Don't forget to invest simultaneously, as time waits for no one. And as I follow, listen, and read about the wealthy they take advantage of time, opportunities, other people's money, work together, and have a mindset to get back up and win when knocked down.

Maximize Your Money

Welcome Wealth

The mindset that it takes to think that you can become wealthy or are wealthy makes people laugh. It's uncomfortable. Try it. **Say**: I am wealthy. I will become wealthy. Did you hesitate? Did you chuckle? More importantly, do you believe it. Now try it out with a close friend or family member and say that you're going to be wealthy one day. What was their response? What was that conversation? I'm curious. Did they chuckle or say something positive or negative? Did they ask you your plans on how you were going to accomplish it? It's awkward thinking about being rich and wealthy as it takes a certain mindset to believe that we have what it takes to become wealthy and see that we are rich in assets. Wealth looks different for every culture because it can be rooted in money, position, power, etc.; whatever the (sub)culture decides is valuable. Your possessions and money may mean nothing to one culture and everything to another. But to ascertain wealth, we first must believe we are capable of achieving wealth. We have to see the vision in our minds. Will you welcome wealth?

Step into your future self with me. You've completed all of the C.A.S.H.F.L.O.W. steps up until this point. At this stage, you would have, or should have:

1. Changed your mindset.
2. Cut emotional spending.
3. Increased your cash flow.
4. Budgeted your money and gutted waste.
5. Developed a tax strategy.
6. Protected your money (insurance & estate planning).
7. Ditched the overspending.
8. Managed your money diligently.
9. Funded a full emergency fund.
10. Taken advantage of investment accounts from your employer or invested in other opportunities.
11. Dominated your credit matters.
12. Crushed your debts.
13. Obtained the deed(s) to your house or other assets.
14. Changed your financial habits to win!
15. Cultivated a circle of like-minded individuals.

And now, you're ready to maximize your investment accounts, maybe even take on educated risks.

How does that sound? Are you excited? That seems so easy, right? Just thinking about it feels like less pressure in life, but doing it is tough. I'm working through them too!

Time to maximize your money in our last step, which takes getting paid interest (compound or in general getting a return on your money) y'all! Compound interest is when your money makes money. It's a defining factor in building wealth. You should be on fire once you get to this stage. I'm dancing in my seat, just thinking about how we're going to turn our world upside down.

You are capable of these tasks. You are deserving of this stage. You are not made for the heavy yoke of being in debt. Jesus paid that price for you! Do not put more on yourself. Strip your mind of your past. Strip your mind of those who keep telling you you can't do it. Strip your mind of negative thoughts. Wipe all of that fear and self-defeating behavior away. You will be victorious! You are a conqueror! (Write that on a sticky note.)

This is the time where if you haven't already secured a financial expert, you need to find one. People have whole teams just to manage their money and invest it. You now have the opportunity to max out retirement accounts if you haven't been doing so at this point, business opportunities look golden, and different types of investments (rental property, trading options on the market, private lending, etc.) can work in your favor because you stayed the course and eliminated the debt. Just know that at this point (at any point really), you want your money making money in a way and rate that's suitable to your timeline and plan.

Side Note: Decide to begin investing earlier as you don't want to miss free money your employer will offer inside a 401K or Employee Stock Plan. Time matters when it comes to doubling your money, so make sure you get with your benefits department and ask them about your investment and retirement options or sign up with a brokerage firm. Let the experts do the work!

Wealthy people make sure that their money is working for them. The bulk of their money is not sitting in a savings or checking account, being depleted by inflation and fees, and earning little to no interest. The wealthy think of ways to make their money grow, and so should you. Remember the banks are leveraging your money everyday.

Here is a list of investment accounts that you may want to consider (not conclusive, just a starter):

Retirement Accounts

Individuals
401(K)
403(B)
457 Plan
Roth IRA
Traditional Individual Retirement Account (IRA)
Self-Directed IRAs

Business Owners
Solo 401(K)
Simplified Employee Pension (SEP-IRA)

Bank Accounts

Certificates of Deposit (CDs)
Money Market Accounts (MMAs)
High-Yield Savings Accounts (HYSA)

Investments Inside Brokerage Accounts

Bonds
Exchange Traded Funds (ETFs)
Stocks
Mutual Funds

Medical Accounts

Health Savings Accounts

Educational Accounts

529 Savings Plan
Coverdell Education Savings Account (ESA)
Savings Bonds

Insurance

Annuities
Long-Term Care Insurance
Private Reserve or Infinite Banking Accounts
Term Life Insurance
Universal Life Insurance
Whole Life Insurance
Variable Life Insurance
Index Universal Life Insurance

Real Assets

Art
Futures and Commodities
Land Banking
Private Businesses
Real Estate (Real Estate Wholesaling, REITs, Real Estate Flipping, Private Lender)

Once you decide on the types of investments you want (you can do that individually or work with an advisor. I say get help!), you need a brokerage account with a firm. Determine if you want full service (estate planning, tax planning, investment planning, and more) or do-it-yourself service. There's a cost for the different levels of service. Do you want VIP, DIY, or a little bit of both? Do you want a human advisor or a set of computed algorithms to help you decide how to invest? Deciding on the type of experience you want and who you trust managing your money will help you figure out where you want to keep your investments. (See Types of Brokerage Firms in the bonus materials).

One thing to keep in mind is that all firms have their policies and way of doing things. They have products that they will recommend, and the advisors that work for them are expected to utilize, push, offer, and sell the products and services. Fiduciary Advisors are still there to look out for your best interest. However, your job as a consumer is to ensure that those products and services are right for you (ask about fees and how your agent is compensated). Another option is to use an independent investment broker to work along-side and connect you to other firms. When hiring anyone to manage your money:

- Don't be afraid to ask questions.
- Never make a decision the first time you meet. (Leave your money purse or wallet behind!
- Always know what actions you're willing to take before you walk into the office or get on the phone.(If you're ready to spend money that day, it's because you have already decided on that action. We have to stop getting bamboozled.)
- If you have a partner, make sure he or she is with you.
- Shop around. You don't have to go with the first person you meet.

You want to make an informed decision, and that can't happen if you don't have time to ask the right questions, chew on it, and discuss it with an accountability partner in a non-pressured environment. We aren't making emotional decisions anymore; we leveled up!

What happens when my investments start making money? The money you make from your investments is called capital gains, and you know that means you gotta pay what? TAXES! Yep, a capital gains tax if you're investing in the stock market! However, some investments have tax advantages, such as insurance policies, even real estate. Know before you invest about different tax structures. It's usually best to consult on such investments with advisors you know,vetted, and trust.

Because you're an informed investor by now (raise the roof), you may be asking your wealth advisors about reinvesting capital gain funds or putting them in tax-free, tax-deferred, or tax-deductible options. Suppose you're investing in stock options that pay dividends quarterly (that's money the company gives its shareholders). In that case, you can automatically reinvest these funds, or you can take it as income (keeping in mind that it's taxed). Some people live off the dividends each year (#goals).

Recall that taxes are your biggest expense. With investments, it's good to know if they will be taxed upfront or on the way out, sometimes never (if you know what you're doing). For example, if you invest in a Roth IRA, your money is taxed upfront, so the money that grows in your account will come out tax-free (aka tax-advantaged). However, in a traditional IRA, taxes are withheld initially, and your money is taxed on the way out (see picture below). Now, suppose you invest in a life insurance policy that will pay out upon your death. In that case, your beneficiary could possibly avoid taxes if setup and distributed appropriately. Wouldn't you want to know the steps to avoid paying taxes? That's why you need a good tax professional and insurance broker in your life. Before you invest, gather how you'll be taxed beforehand (no tax surprises); always assess your risks.

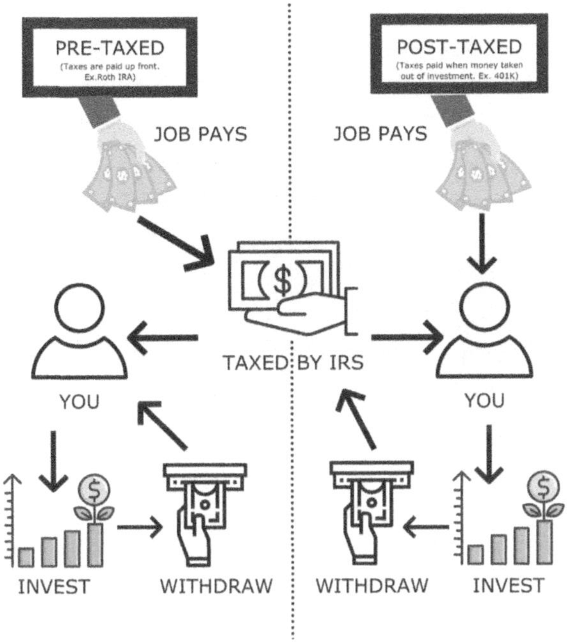

What happens when I need to pull money from my investment? Many investments have stipulations. When I invest, I think long-term. Can some investments be short-term investments? Yes, but when you're building wealth that *sticks to your ribs*, you want to think long-term (Don't confuse day trading with investing.). Taking money out from certain investments, like retirement accounts, before the time it matures or the rules say you can result in penalties (tax penalties and fees) and disrupts the progress you made and could make while investing. Do you really want to give up 10% of your money? Investments such as 401K's and 403B's, bonds, certificates of deposits (CDs), and IRAs have such penalties for pulling your money out early.

Some investment types are set up to counter such penalties and losses, like the self-banking concept through insurance policies. I will only mention it so that you're in the know about such options. Ask a trusted insurance agent to find out more information. It's an intriguing concept as alternate idea of get term insurance and then invest the rest. There are many wealth-building strategies. What matters most is that you work with credible experts who will help you build a portfolio according to your goals and risk tolerance.

Before investing, please make sure you understand the assets or securities you purchase: how it works, how it benefits you, the fees associated with managing it, and how the money pays out upon your retirement and death.

Now we all know trouble comes a knockin' you may *want* or *need* to borrow from your retirement accounts. Some circumstances allow you to borrow from your retirement accounts penalty-free, but you should tread very carefully when borrowing from accounts you have set aside for your future. Nearly 9 out of 10 times, stealing from your future is not a wise decision. If I could write to my younger self and tell myself a piece of advice, what lesson would it be? I'd advise myself to keep my investments and avoid selling them for hard times (let me correct that–for gifts, lack of planning, and hard times. SMH!). I had the intention of doing the right thing at times, but it spiraled out of control. I don't want you to make the same mistake I made. I'd like to believe that most advisors will tell you that it's not a good decision, but life throws us some nasty blows. At this point in your journey, you should be a more mature and fiscally responsible person. You will know to seek wise counsel if you were up against a wall.

I know life happens, but don't risk your future for temporary situations. Should severe and unforeseeable events occur, having a fully established emergency fund *can* mitigate *some* of life's hardships. We know that there are some situations that only God can carry you through. Money is a tool–it can only do what it's meant to do.

Even now you may be inspired by what others are investing into. Be cautious and not presumptuous. Your path and financial makeup may be different. Be diligent and make wise choices about where you invest your money. Sometimes, we view other's successes as mere whims, but the time and effort in calculating wins are not executed on impulse. Get familiar with the behind scenes plays, so you can be well informed if the investment is for you.

Who Should Be On My Money Team

Throughout your journey, you should be reading and educating yourself. Your bonus materials will have a list of financial literacy book suggestions. You've already started here, so now keep learning! While educating yourself, don't forget to surround yourself with financial experts. There's a famous quote in the direct sales industry that says, "Success loves speed," and if you want to be successful and fast, create a team of people around your vision.

Such a team includes a financial advisor. Education and experience matter when you're trying to grow your money, so getting someone more informed than yourself is a grand idea. Understand that advisors should work on your behalf while satisfying the entity in which they work (if they represent a firm). Though they will get a kickback for offering certain products, you still get to your money goal. It's a give-and-take relationship, but how much are you willing to give up? Note that financial advisors are not equal (goes for any profession). Make sure you prepare some questions: How will they get paid? Fee based or commission based? Another question in mind is to find out if your advisor is a fiduciary? Again, a fiduciary must do what is in the best interest for the customer. You might ask their education and experience along with other questions such as what products they recommend and why? What is their philosophy when it comes to investing? Put them in the hot seat! The more questions you ask, the more you know. You'll be able to identify if this is someone you can work with long-term. You have to interview the people that you want to handle your money.

The person who gets the better deal is the one who is most informed.

Having some knowledge is better than none when you are dealing with your finances. I've heard enough stories of people nearly getting robbed at the car dealership with predatory loans. In many instances, car buyers who are financially literate exercise their rights by leaving the office, and walking towards the exit because the agent refuses to make a better offer. These individuals know they have every right to avoid such low terms because they know their numbers (interest rates, credit scores, etc.). If the salesman knows what's good for them, they'll stop you and make a better offer before you leave. Put your knowledge into action–negotiate and don't be afraid to walk away from the table.

The same goes for building wealth. I was in a seminar, and the financial advisor relayed a personal experience she had with a client. The advisor was passionate about women understanding their role in relationships when it comes to finances. Many times women are uninformed about the financial situation in their marriages. To continue, she was trying to help a client whose husband had died. They'd been under the same plan with another company, and after evaluating it, the numbers showed that the agent was getting a fat check from the client's investment portfolio. (The client was now a widow, and her husband had set up the account. She did not know anything about the investment.) And because she didn't understand, she stayed with the advisor rather than saving tens of thousands of dollars with the advisor who showed her exactly why her investment plan was terrible (the fees attached were astronomical). The other company used longevity and the fact that her husband "*trusted*" them to keep the symbiotic partnership going. Uggh! Addiction to familiarity and a lack of financial education will keep you in bad financial relationships (any relationship). I've stayed in toxic relationships because of loyalty. It's time to break up. Don't be afraid to *chunk the deuce*, and keep it rolling!

Don't get me wrong, financial advisors are phenomenal and there to help you build wealth. I use them too! You need to be informed enough and interested enough to know when you're getting the short end of a deal. As mentioned above, the advisor tried to educate the client but was unsuccessful. The firm offered to evaluate the situation for free, showed the client where she was losing money, and then gave the client advice on how they could grow their money. If any of us had someone to analyze our financial portfolios as such, we could make an informed decision about whether or not we would move forward; that's a win-win situation to me! If you're skeptical, get a second opinion.

Another person you want in your corner (at all times), especially when you begin to build wealth, is a tax professional (the planners). These individuals differ as well. You have Enrolled Agents, Certified Public Accountants, Non-certified tax preparers, Tax Attorneys, and Annual Filing Season Participants (see bonus material for additional information about the different types). As always, you need to ask questions as well. Not all tax professionals are equal.

These professionals can help you avoid costly taxes that come with having and making more money. They can help you plan for the upcoming year and make sure you keep more of your coins! Remember, we live in a capitalistic society. If you don't know the rules, you can't effectively play the game. So let the experts do the work they do because tax laws change and update throughout the year. And don't forget to inform yourself in this area as well. A good tax professional will answer your questions and keep their ear to the ground about new tax laws to help their clients. Work with your tax professional to create a strategic plan to keep more money in your pocket.

Other professionals include insurance brokers, Realtor, car salesman, estate attorney, consumer attorney, bookkeeper, registered investment agent, someone skilled in health insurance, and any other expert in the area that you're involved. Decide if you want to build your team or go with a full firm to manage your wealth.

* * *

One question you want to **redefine** at this stage may be: What does financial freedom look like to you? What do you want your financial responsibilities to be when you retire? What dollar amount will be sufficient for your retirement?

When I began on this journey, the world taught us that you retire at age 65. But when I started shifting my mindset and shaping my circle of influence, retirement was not about my age; it quickly became apparent that it's about the dollar amount and a decision that helps you to live financially comfortably until you move beyond this world.

Take a moment and write this statement. I will be financially free when I can _______________ and have _______________ to live off of monthly for the rest of my life. (Note: with all that's going on this could be difficult to answer, but start somewhere.)

Retirement questions to consider: Ask yourself how much you need monthly to survive. How long do you need your money to last? What investments can help you generate enough money monthly or yearly to live off without touching the initial investment? What do you want to do during retirement (travel, volunteer, philanthropic ventures, etc.)? Who will take care of you? Healthcare coverage? A financial advisor and estate planner can help you prepare for retirement.

I often hear people say, "I'm going to work until I can't," or "I'm working till I die," and there's nothing wrong with that notion ... Well, just a *teenie* bit! First, let's be honest, it's a blessing to be able to work and move around physically and be in our right minds during retirement (especially if we're up in age). On the other hand, some absolutely love what they do and feel like it is their calling. I get it. I love working with kids, and that's the problem with education! Educators love what they do, and will sacrifice their life.

But for others, what else can you do during retirement that you can't do at someone else's establishment, or even your own establishment, if you weren't tied down? Think of the possibilities. We won't be here forever, so we need to make sure to prepare the generation we're leaving to handle the resources we'll be leaving behind as well as enjoy ourselves and create precious moments! We missed a lot time overworking. Hopefully, you would've done this throughout your life, but think of your dreams, your God dreams!

Retirement doesn't mean that you sit idle for the rest of your years. It's a way to do more of what you want because you *have* put in the work. I don't suggest being idle by any means because that's a sure way to our demise. We *work* on what's meaningful and more impactful in our later years if we haven't done so beforehand. What if you could do more through retirement when your schedule is free than you ever could have while working? Think about the assignment God has for you or the passion project you've wanted to complete. We really don't retire. There's just *other work* to be done. However, we should try to see the benefits of having this time. It may be spending more time with family, volunteering for a cause you're passionate about, getting to know our mates on a deeper level during this period (you've probably changed over the years), experiencing the world like never before, impacting lives through philanthropy projects, or even working part-time. When I talk to my friends, we dream of being lenders, owning an orphanage, helping children, and many other opportunities. My ultimate goal is to be a vessel for children, social justice, literacy, economic power, and mental health. Think about working where and when you want (or not at all) instead of working because you have to—that's freedom.

In some professions, like education, walking away can be difficult. But how our gifts could explode if we had 100% of our working hours to do them! Lives can be changed. Hurts can be healed. Souls can be saved, y'all! Your mind and time are your most precious commodities. Work till you die at someone else's place of employment? Ahh nah! "Work till you die" was written upon the entrance of the Auschwitz concentration camp—work sets you free, "*Arbeit Macht Frei*." Except this work was meant to kill you: It translated to, "in death is where you'd find your freedom." Extermination through work was the practice, "*Vernichtung durch arbeit*." That's the mindset we've adopted. Don't get me wrong, again; there's honor in working. *And* there's honor outside of your job, too! Believers, we know that we have work here to be done for the reward now and later!

I pray your life experiences will be seasoned. I urge you to enjoy the fruits of your labor, impart your wisdom to those around you, plant seeds for the Kingdom, and leave behind a trail of goodness so thick that it's inspiring and uplifting! You're replaceable at your job because you have to be—it's designed that way. However, there's different work you need to complete throughout your lifetime and during your final chapters, which is irreplaceable and has lasting effects. The people you're charged with caring for and loving can experience you on a whole new level.

Once you are at the wealth-building stage, don't forget to redo your budget to fit your investment plans. You may be tempted to spend lavishly, but I caution you to stay the course and build your legacy. You may even increase your giving. **Note**: You still need to have a plan for your money! Because this is also a time where predators are looking to reap where they did not sow, robbing you of your hard work and your beneficiaries of their inheritance. Be vigilant to keep trustworthy people around you.

Experts say that you spend more money during the last six years of your life than in any other decade of your life due to healthcare costs. Because our cost of living rises we need to be aware of debt. We don't want to take on any if we don't have to. If we're not financially prepared for this time period nor consult with experts we may make mistakes where we might lose our homes, take on a bad investment, reluctantly return to work, or lose our independence. So plan your money as best as you are able. Spend what you can *really* afford, and when you can't, wait. The responsibility is up to you.

How do we protect our investments? While investing and building your legacy, you will ensure that you protect your assets by establishing some instructions such as a living will, will, setting up a revocable or irrevocable trust at the proper time, etc. (find an estate planner) and add beneficiaries to all of your accounts, updating each yearly.

Hopefully, before this point, you have established these documents. Make sure you update or review your directives yearly or whenever major changes happen. A will gives directions to your loved ones about what to do with your possessions (but it may not stop you from going to probate court, so an estate planner is necessary). Once you acquire assets, you need to protect your assets.

If you're wealthy or own anything of importance, you can set aside instructions to leave specific assets to others. Remember that emergencies happen, and you should be prepared. Hopefully, the wealth you build will be enough to last beyond your lifetime once you stop actively working, leaving behind whatever you desire to family, friends, or organizations. I'm not mad at you if you decide to dedicate funds to care for your furbaby!

I encourage you to think about how your money can outlive you and impact the next generation. Statistics show that wealth lasts longer (several generations) when created within families. My view is that the family is the crux of wealth building. Families create wealth that sticks to your ribs. But don't expect your wealth to have lasting effects if you never educate those coming after you. You must create and teach the habits and posture that it takes to build and keep the wealth of those who will succeed you. So singles, we have to be strategic here. Where will our wealth go, and how can we ensure that it lasts beyond our years?

Make sure your will, living will, last wishes, trust funds, beneficiaries, insurance policies, and more are properly established and updated. To do so:

1. Find a skilled attorney and estate planner to help you draw up these essential documents (get them signed and notarized). Don't leave a tragic situation more devastating without having the proper

paperwork in place. (Side note: check your benefits to see if you have free services that will help you create your will or offer estate planning at a reduced price. Many people miss out on employer benefits because they never explore resources from their HR department).

2. Begin researching your options. The older you get, the more vulnerable you are to scams trying to monetize from your hard work. Protect your assets. And make sure you have a living will so that you assign a guardian of your choice if you are left incapacitated. You do not want the government to assign court-appointed guardians that could expose your wealth to vultures and leave you and your family dry. That's why good family members are essential to keep around.
3. Don't forget to educate those around you both about the legacy you want them to leave and about your final instructions. Find the person or persons who will carry the torch.
4. Imperatively, make sure you have updated your beneficiaries! I can't tell you how many stories I've heard where the money went to someone it was no longer intended for because the beneficiaries were outdated. Look at yours now!

What plan will you put in place for your legacy and wealth to last? Remember,

Everyone has a plan for your money. Do you?

Build your legacy by educating yourself, setting aside proper funds, surrounding yourself with other legacy builders, and utilizing financial experts. Success takes a community, and you want to be able to share it with others. Legacy is not just about money. It requires an enriched character and routines that will outlast money. But by all means: Make your money, manage your money, and maximize your money!

So, get
ready, light
your flame,
and ignite
your.
Spark!

The Beginning

You made it to the beginning (yes, the beginning) of your personal financial chapter! I hope you're brimming with ideas and excited to get started or continue your financial journey. Your transformation happens when you take one step forward and maintain a steady pace down the path to recover your emotional, mental, and financial health. However, if you fail to make changes, you will continue to be in the same predicament. Keep going, and never quit!

Choose to take care of your stressors, go to work for you, and fight against the norm of society when it comes to finances. Just know that this journey is as tricky as your mindset envisions it. You will make mistakes. You will take several steps back. You may even have to start over! I still make mistakes and have plenty of roadblocks I've yet to encounter! Remember, your success is directly related to your mindset. Permit yourself to forgive yourself so that you can move toward your financial goals.

As you're working on your mindset, figure out what your real issues are so you can get to the root of the problems and begin to target those areas. I had to understand that my self-worth, pleasing tendencies, passiveness, and avoiding conflict were the roots of my problem. Whew! I sound like a whole case, but it was only with this knowledge I could move forward.

Figure out your money-related reactions to stress: Are you spending to numb your situation? As you begin to dig deep, have a growth mindset. Don't expect to arrive at your destination quickly. It took you months, years, and decades to develop your mindset and debt, so it will take some time to eliminate stress and destructive financial habits. Moreover, take time to get your emotions in check. Children act by way of feelings. You can't take care of the critical areas of your life by making emotional decisions. You're an adult, and feeling your way through life is childish. It's time to shed that skin and be proactive, not reactive.

Lastly, to get our mindset under lock, we should practice some form of meditation. Whether you read the Bible, listen to instrumental music, repeat affirmative mantras, sit in quiet, go outside with nature, etc., take time to center yourself. The goal is to relax on the one hand but also to seek clarity through meditation and stillness. The two are different. Relaxation may include some stimuli, but meditation requires silence and zero to minimal outside stimuli. Be intentional about these *Ummm* moments and make them a part of your routine. The most important part of your health is your mental health. Only then will everything else be in alignment.

On your journey, don't forget the other key steps to find your spark:

1. Target your success. Making goals is key to your success in any area of your life. If you only think about it, it's a wish. You must plan, write it down, and execute.
2. Solicit the help of others. Find trustworthy and reliable players in your life that will allow you to talk out your problems without repercussions. You need a good shoulder to lean on, whether it's a friend or seeking professional help. Avoid underestimating the rewards of having caring and trusting confi dants.

3. Avoid tempting situations that come to rob you of your well-being. These could be objects, such as food, events, activities, or people who drain your energy. We have to be proactive and know what's good for us before we walk into situations that cause us to be stressed and spend money irrationally. To avoid temptation, you have to know yourself and be cognitive of the factors that aren't in your best interest. To combat such temptations, we have to be strategic about who and what we invite into our lives. Opt to volunteer or begin a project to take the focus off of your stress. Subscribe to people and places that align with your goals. And if you're using social media heavily, make sure you shape your timeline (and email) to match what you're looking for in your life.
4. The word control has many negative connotations, but without it, we live wild lives with little ambition but to satisfy our physical needs and wants. It is necessary to control our lives and get rid of our stress and financial woes by eliminating the self-aimed negative thoughts. Take time to decompress and rejuvenate, so you don't get overwhelmed. It's during these times of anxiety we often have negative thoughts. We have to take control of our voice and say *no* to ourselves and others. We must organize and plan our steps: Using a calendar, technology, and making lists help us to stay organized. Prioritizing what we need to do helps us stay on track with our goals. We MUST tell our money where to go! We need to take control of our minds, voices, time, and money to keep our crowns on straight.

Once we have control over these areas, conquering our finances will just be a matter of execution. We have to remember that money is a tool, much like a screwdriver. Use it with such precision that it gets the tasks done that you aim for. When we take the emotions out of our finances, we can see our financial world more clearly. We can see how our employers, government, taxes, budgets, debt, credit, compound interest, emergency funds, and wills all work together. It's a well-orchestrated dance when you know how it all works and how you and your money fit into the ensemble.

We can't control most things in this world, but we can control our thoughts and our action. Take captive every thought and submit to the Almighty. *Humans make their plans*, but God directs our path (Proverbs 16:9).

From this point on, I want you to give yourself a winning chance with your money. Lay down the stressors. Pick up the habits you need to win with money, and crush every goal you set! Reread this book by yourself or with a friend, and work through it as a journal. Read a section and work on that section. Write down your thoughts, your goals, and your dreams. Feel free to share your successes and questions with me at info@rashidaroberts.com. Don't forget to download your resources at bonus.findyourspark.info.

Make sure to keep yourself surrounded by others going in the direction you want to go, as they will not only be a balm in time of need, they'll inspire you to go further than you imagined. Plus you'll get inside tips.

Be vigilant, my dear friends, to avoid the pitfalls of this world. As you acquire more and become financially free, the glitter and gold will be tempting. It is easy to fall back down into old habits and forget all of the hard work you put in on your journey. Put this quote on a sticky note:

The world will teach you how to get into debt. Your family and friends will encourage your debt. And the creditors will profi t from your debt until you have the courage to say NO!

People and organizations will be vying for your money. Don't give them a foothold. Stay diligent. Stay educated. Keep good company. Give, give, give to the organizations, the poor, your Church, and people that are dear to your heart. And leave your legacy.

Remember the Commission you've been charged with, the purpose you have been given, and the people you've been rooted near. The time is now.

Take a moment to assess where you are in your journey and figure out your next steps. Do you have the mindset, and are you ready to tackle your finances, or do you need to get your mind right first to set the stage for your financial goals? Either way: Start somewhere, and the rest will come.

Let's crush debt together and celebrate every win!

You have the tools you need, so go out there and light your match. It only takes a spark to transform your world!

Courageously, do the unimaginable!

"It only takes a spark to light up a whole fores
Take the first step and light your world on fire!"
RaShida Roberts

About the Author

First and foremost, RaShida Roberts is the daughter of the Most High God. After graduating from the University of Houston in 2004, she became an educator in 2006. Soon after, she enrolled in her graduate program in 2008 to better assist her students through technology. RaShida's graduate degree is from Full Sail University in Instructional Design & Technology in 2019. She is an educator of fifteen years and has worked in elementary and middle school and online for four of those years. She was named the Rookie Teacher of the Year, nominated at least five times for Teacher of the Year, and in 2016, was voted the Most Inspirational Teacher of the Year, working virtually. She continues to work as an educator in every aspect of her life.

RaShida has had training in crisis support, child advocacy (as an ad litem for CPS and through her education profession), and has volunteered with her church for many years as an American Sign Language (ASL) Interpreter (songs and scripture), small group instructor, Sunday School teacher, and VBS coordinator. She has volunteered with organizations such as KSBJ, Target Hunger, Child Advocate, and the public schools she has served. Children, abuse, education, mental health awareness, financial literacy, social justice, and her faith are her top personal concerns and areas she supports for partnerships. She is the owner of Target Financial, a financial service and consultant company delivering financial literacy and content to help people change their relationship with money through financial coaching, partnerships with financial experts, and educational workshops.

RaShida's book, *Find Your Spark: 7 Steps to Ditch Stress and Ignite Your Financial Lifestyle,* is her entry into the financial literacy domain. Continually educating herself, she became a certified Board Credit Consultant (2020) by the Credit Consultants Association and has received her Master Financial Coaching certificate to support her future financial coaching clients. She is a volunteer Financial Coach with Eden Housing, Inc. empowering residents to build long-term financial health and stability. RaShida is helping singles and educators crush their debt and move toward financial independence. To work with RaShida and find her on all social media platforms, visit www.thecashflowconvo.com. If you're interested in ditching debt, reach out to become a part of a movement of people refusing to live life on others' terms.

She believes, "*The more control we have over our finances helps us to find our unique voice*." Follow RaShida Roberts on her debt-free journey to impact the lives of those around her as she uses her voice to educate, educate, educate, and help people start their journey to financial freedom.

Acknowledgements

I want to personally thank the individuals and small business owners who supported this book before the words even existed! Please take time to visit their pages and connect with them. They have provided their information along with a personal quote in hopes to inspire you on your journey! Let's make our villages bigger and better by supporting each other!

Alicia Richards
"*The most common way people give up their power is by thinking they don't have any.*" Alice Walker

Andrea Wilson
Owner
www.QueenBlingJewelry.Online
"*Strategy is Important, but execution is everything.*"

Brandy Black
Senior Accountant
LinkedIn: @brandyblack
"*Do what you NEED to do so you can do what WANT to do!*"

Rev. Beverly Roberts
Author and Reverend
Instagram: @rbdroberts
"*God first in all things.*"

Chanel Spencer
Branding Visionary
www.readytotransformnow.com
"Your past circumstances do not have control of your present or determine your future success."

Chelise Manuel
Mentor, Business Owner
Instagram: @deches_customcreationz *"Live life with no regrets."*

Chernika L Corbett
CEO, DéJa Vu Skin
www.dejavuskin.com
"I decided I'm going to stop being sad and be a goddess of love and light. A queen of resilience and power, and a warrior of bold fearlessness. Straighten my crown and conquer."

Dr. Holly Barnett-Brown
Director of Education Success
LinkedIn: @holly-brown-938b9692
"Your joy is your decision."

Jassy Dallas Childs
CEO, Baking Fabulista
www.fabulistacookies.com
"The way you manage your time lets me know if you are worth me investing my constructed time with you. Money can be replaced, but never can lost time. It is our greatest, irreplaceable commodity."

Judy Gaskin
www.sweatnstyle.com
"Make each day better than the [last]."

Mary Ann Adams
CEO, On T.R.A.C.K. Ministry
"Life is really like a box of chocolates, some sweet and smooth, as life can be good to you; some bitter, like the challenges we face in life; and some nutty, like some of the nutty people we encounter. So, as we enjoy our chocolates, let us enjoy this life...only one box."

Dr. Octavius Sanders
"Live life to the fullest and help others along the way!"

Queen Paula Kent
Minister
FB: prettiestblackno1
"My life had to happen the way it did so that I'd become the woman of God I am today!!"

Sunjanel Avecilla
Senior Consultant
MPCG Medical Consultants

Tammie T. Polk
Goal and Dream Fulfillment Coach
www.professionallysassy.me
"Just because someone does what you do doesn't mean they do what YOU do!"

Yvonne Brown
Financial Coach
http://www.yvonnebrownexhales.com
"You have to be willing to make a short-term sacrifice for a greater financial gain."

To those of you

who are hidden, silent, struggling to find

your voice, suffering in silence, selflessly giving of

themselves, and who have been treated and convicted

wrongly by no fault of their own. And to those who are

fighting every day to put on the new self, to make it,

to smile, to encourage others, to help the underserved,

to protect and to serve where honor is lacking,

and to put on the whole armor of God

in the face of hatred,

to my

Believers:

I

salute

you.

Take a Peek...

Poetry Excerpt from *Step Into Your Power*,
co-authored by RaShida Roberts

Order your copy:
http://siypwithme.thecashflowconvo.com

I AM
ENOUGH!
The walking cotton threads shout.
I glow with confidence
Convincing everyone about.
Juxtapose and jagged
Is my walk.
My life in other's hands:
perfection I stalk.
The road to destruction
To put it on the line
When they are pleased,
My heart is divine.
What life is that to live?
To be such a puppet.
To give yourself away,
Left ragged and then plummet,
Down to another's decision On your day-to-day work. You run yourself in circles Pleasing their quirks.
They take and take
They gollop you whole.
But remember,
You signed the dotted lines To be included in such a toll.
Enough is enough.
Can you escape the damage?
You never stood for yourself
They got the advantage. Now you reminisce
And scoff at your acts.
You can't be enough
You let them treat you like that?
I AM ENOUGH!
I shout to these walls.
I've stammered enough
In darkness I've crawled.
I can bear no more
Of self-defeating behavior
The line is thin
failure or savior?
Just a few words
Of hope and em-powerment.
I say to myself
Each day for betterment.
The mountains have sunken
In size when I see,
The view from a different
Vantage point of glee.

My power is
between my ears.
Controlling my thoughts
Decreasing my fears.

Now I say:
I AM ENOUGH
For all I encounter.

I AM ENOUGH
Because I've stepped into my POWER!

Appears in the book *Step Into Your Power* by visionary, Teasha Ross

Discussion Questions

Chapter 1

Explain how hard it is to forget the past and forgive yourself. Why is it important to take this step? Do you think our past mistakes dictate our money habits? Why or why not?

How can our past money issues show up in our daily lives?

The author suggests that we need to get down to the root cause of our financial stress. What area should you target?

How does stress show up in our financial lives?

What deep issues do you need to resolve to handle your financial life better?

How are you getting in your way when it comes to your financial lifestyle?

What one habit is stopping you from living your best financial life right now?

How do you react to stress-related events?

How well does your money hold up during stressful times?

What roadblocks are you setting up to curb some of your bad habits?

How do you spend your money when you are stressed?

Who do you allow in your life to give you a dose of reality without the love, respect, or relationship declining?

Who's stepping in to stop you from your harmful reactions to stress?

How does negative thinking get in the way of our financial goals and stress?

What can positive thinking and a growth mindset do for you? What will it take for you to start thinking in such a way?

Who is the most positive person in your life to help you with being more positive about your situation?

Who do you know that displays a growth mindset? What characteristics does this person have or display?

Explain a time you allowed your emotions to dictate your life. What would you do differently?

How are our emotions tied to stress? How are they connected to money?

The author suggests writing as a form of healing. Have you tried to write or dictate your emotions to help you discuss issues in your life? Why or why not?

How can removing yourself from negative situations help decrease stress or help you avoid financial pitfalls?

Do you agree that avoiding certain scenarios is best when stressed or in a financial crisis? Why or why not?

How can our environment affect our stress levels? How can our environment affect our financial lifestyle?

What form of meditation do you practice to decrease stress? Is it working? Why or why not? How often should one practice meditation and decompressing?

In what ways do you need to show up for yourself when it comes to mindset and removing stress?

Chapter 2

Some people suggest that you don't always need a goal to be successful, and that by going here and there, you will find your purpose. This author suggests targeting your success and setting goals. Do you believe having such goals would help one relieve stress and help to establish better financial habits?

What goals have you set as a result of reading this chapter?

What can you change about your current situation that would advocate for a less stressful or financially stable life? What are you willing to do to get there?

Thinking about the future can be overwhelming. What does the author suggest we do to take care of what-ifs in our lives? Do you agree or disagree? Why or why not?

How do you prepare for possible future disasters?

What can people do to prepare for common emergencies?

How do you bounce back from an emergent situation to avoid becoming stressed? What suggestions would you give to others based on this book or your own opinions?

Why is it important for people to have a vision and write it down? Is journaling needed to conquer goals?

In your opinion, why is writing important or not important when targeting success in key areas of your life? What does the author say about it that stuck out to you? Are there any statements that you agree or disagree with in the book about writing your vision down?

Should we celebrate the small wins in our lives as we achieve our goals? Why or why not?

Share a win that you have had in the area of stress and your finances. How does it make you feel?

Chapter 3

How important is it for us to choose our circle wisely?

Name three people that you can absolutely go to and discuss any issue with without judgment. What about them makes them quality confidants for you?

Are you able to trust others? Why or why not?

The author believes that it is essential to talk with others about stressful situations. Do you agree or disagree with this notion?

Name some trusted friends or wise counsel that you can talk to about your finances and stress.

How can going outside of your immediate circle help you gain new ideas about overcoming stress and developing better financial habits? Is this something that you are prepared to do? Why or why not?

How often do you ask for help when you are overwhelmed? Do you feel that asking for help is weak? Why or why not?

Most people choose to suffer in silence. Why do you think this is so?

List people in each area of your life that you could connect with and ask for support.

What do you think it would take for people to humble themselves and ask for help?

Name three things that you need to be brutally honest about.

How and why do we lie to ourselves? Do you think this perpetuates our stress and financial issues?

Mental health is a rising and prevalent topic. Do you believe that it would help people to talk to a professional counselor about their stress and financial issues? Why or why not?

What are some hesitations that keep people from seeing a mental health provider? Do you have a problem with going to a professional? Explain.

How important is it to listen as much as it is to talk when dealing with stress?

Who was the last person you listened to? And what did you find out?

How can you improve your listening skills?

Chapter 4

How do temptations exacerbate our stressful situations and financial lifestyle?

What areas of temptation do you need to avoid or eliminate from your life to be successful?

Do you believe it's essential for people to limit stressful situations? Or should people face their stressful situations head-on to overcome their obstacles? Explain why or why not.

How can we prevent ourselves from going into stressful situations?

How can we prevent ourselves from being in environments which solicit us to spend our money?

Sometimes we cannot choose who is in proximity to us. How then can we carefully select who to adopt into our private circles?

What characteristics does a quality person have to possess for you to invite them into your most private and intimate spaces?

In the world of social media, explain why it is vital for us to shape our timelines to reveal more of what we want in our life.

Do you feel social media has an impact on our psyche? Does it impact our stress levels or financial habits? Explain your answer.

What limits or boundaries do you need to set when it comes to social media?

How can people be more proactive about eliminating temptations on social media?

There's a saying that you should never burn a relationship but build a bridge. The author suggests that you need to burn the bridges of toxicity. Do you agree or disagree? Why or why not?

What are some characteristics of toxic people? Do you have any such people in your life? If so, how do you plan to rid yourself of such people? Why or why not?

What is the best way to deal with a toxic person? What is the best way to deal with a toxic person that cannot escape?

Have you ever been in a toxic situation? What advice would you give to someone about unhealthy relationships and the stress that they cause?

How can boundaries help you to avoid toxic situations?

Are boundaries needed when it comes to building financial habits? Why or why not?

Name some healthy boundaries that would facilitate less stress and better financial habits.

What boundaries do you need to set in your life?

What toxic habits do you have that need to be removed, so you can deal with or lower your stress levels?

Are there any unhealthy relationships that need removing or fixing in your life? Explain.

Chapter 5

To straighten your crown and take control of your stress and finances, the author suggests that one should get rid of negative thoughts, find their voice and say no, get organized, and start telling their money where to go. Which area do you feel you need to gain control to deal with your life's stress and financial issues?

How often do you believe people replay negative conversations in their heads? Do you think these thoughts are helpful or harmful to one's lifestyle?

How successful are people who constantly think negatively?

What benefits do thinking more positively have on one's life?

In what ways will positive thinking decrease stress and help one to develop positive financial practices?

What can you say to deter yourself from thinking negatively?

How often do you say no? Why or why not?

How does being a people pleaser or perfectionist affect stress? And how can it affect our financial practices?

How do the opinions of others affect us financially? How do the opinions of others affect our stress levels?

Why should or shouldn't people take an approach of saying no more often? Do you think saying no is a healthy practice? Why or why not?

Where in your life do you need to speak up and say no?

What are the consequences of saying no?

How can getting organized help you take control over your stress and financial lifestyle?

What tip from the book are you willing to try to stay organized? What advice do you have about staying organized? How do you feel when you are organized?

Why is it important to take control of our money?

What is one way you can take control of your money and tell your money where to go? What does the author suggest about this topic? Do you agree or disagree?

How do you feel about speaking with an expert to help you take control of your finances? Do you think a financial expert could help you? If so, in what areas? Who would you seek out? If not, why? What would stop you from seeking professional help?

Do you feel people are hesitant to talk to financial experts? Why or why not?

We find an expert for every area of our lives. Think about your hair, nails, medical, car, home, education, etc., and others you seek to help you with your issues. Why don't more people use experts for their financial matters? What do you feel is the cause of this, and what can be done?

What's your first step to straightening your crown and taking control over your stress and finances?

Chapter 6

How important is it that we manage our time?

Do you overcommit yourself? If so, in what areas?

How does overcommitting ourselves lead to stress and financial ruin?

What goals do you need to set around overcommitting? What actions will you take to accomplish your goals?

What tip from Chapter 6 do you already use or would use to help streamline your time?

How do you prioritize what needs to get done in your life?

What are some items and tasks that keep you busy? Which tasks do you need to eliminate?

How important is planning your time? Do you feel planning can help you become stress-free, debt-free, or have a better relationship? Why or why not?

How important is it to allow flexibility in your goals?

How do you feel when you have setbacks?

How do setbacks affect our stress levels? What can we do about it?

What distracts you from using your time wisely? What can you do to eliminate distractions?

What distractions have you had when it comes to living your dream life?

The term self-care is at an all-time high. Do you make time for decompressing? Why or why not?

Is self-care necessary to maximize our time? Explain.

List some ways that you decompress or are willing to try after reading this chapter.

How will self-care help you ditch stress? How will it help you to make better choices with your finances?

What is your greatest hindrance to managing your time? What steps do you need to take to fix this problem?

Chapter 7

How has your financial life evolved over your lifetime? Is what you're doing now working for your betterment? Explain.

Do you feel that more money will help people manage their finances better? Explain.

Discuss your saving habits. What helps you or stops you from being successful in this area?

What percentage of money do you save each year?

What are your financial goals?

Would you consider yourself a good steward over your money?

What does financial freedom mean to you?

The author suggests making one financial decision at a time. Do you agree or disagree? Where would you start? Where should people in general start on their financial journey?

How important is it to change your mindset when it comes to conquering your financial goals?

What and who influences our financial mindsets?

Who taught you about money growing up as a child? And what did they teach you?

What do you believe about money?

What challenges have you had with money as an adult?

How does money affect your relationships?

How do you feel when you have enough money? How do you feel when you don't have enough money?

If you've borrowed money before, how did it make you feel asking someone for it?

Are you able to talk openly about money? Why or why not?

Who can you actually talk to about money? Honestly, how does it feel to talk about money?

Does your partner feel the same as you do about money? How important is money in your relationship?

Are you capable of teaching your kids or someone you know about money?

Do you feel you can give without regrets to others with your money situation?

How do you feel about others borrowing money from you?

Do you give to charity? Why or why not?

Does someone owe you money? How does that feel?

Where does most of your money go?

How does spending money make you feel? Why do you think it makes you feel this way?

Do you make enough money? Why or why not?

In what ways could you make more money?

What three things get in the way for you to be financially stable?

Have you thought about retirement? What will you use for retirement funds?

What will happen, financially, to your loved ones if you pass suddenly? Will they have enough money to live comfortably?

What philosophy do you hold about money as it relates to generational wealth?

If you lost all of your money, what would you do?

How should you invest your money?

Is there someone helping you with your finances? If not, how is that working out? If so, who and why did you choose them or that entity?

According to the author, why is it not a good idea to leave large sums of money in a regular banking account? Do you agree or disagree? Why?

Which of the four financial challenges are you most concerned about: big business, inflation, taxes, or debt? How will you make changes to overcome these four challenges?

The author suggests that people need to stop getting a refund on their tax returns. What are your thoughts about this idea?

What in this chapter stood out the most?

Are you overpaying in taxes? Why or why not?

Based on the ideas presented in the book, what are some ways to minimize your tax obligation, legally?

What is emotional spending, and how often do you do it?

How can emotional spending be debtrimental to our financial goals?

How can we curve our emotional spending?

Which area in the C.A.S.H.F.L.O.W. method do you need to spend time developing?

Many financial experts recommend writing a budget. Do you feel this is a strategy worth spending time on or not? Why?

What do you believe about budgets?

Share some positive outcomes on using a budget.

The author is a firm believer in building a quick and full emergency fund. How can an emergency fund help you or others? What hindrances do you foresee in establishing an emergency fund?

Which tips will you utilize to fill your pockets and keep more of your money?

Many people are focused on their credit scores, but the author suggests they should be focused on their debt first. What are your thoughts?

How does credit affect your financial lifestyle?

What tips did you learn about credit, and which ones will you act upon?

Do you have a debt-free date? Why or why not?

What are you willing to sacrifice to be debt-free?

How important is getting a house to you? Why?

The author feels that there is no good debt. Debt is debt. Do you think that a house is a good or bad debt? Why?

How does it feel to juggle debt?

Many financial experts say to leverage your credit cards, and some are totally against using credit. What are your thoughts on the topic?

Is it okay to pay for overpriced items simply because you can afford the bill? Should we be living as such? Why or why not?

What does it mean to be wealthy? Do you believe you can get to a wealthy status? Why or why not?

Have you started building wealth? Share the areas you have begun to build wealth.

Insurance is a vehicle to building wealth. Do you have a life insurance policy? What are your thoughts about getting insurance to leave for your family?

Which wealth-building ideas will you research further?

Do you feel you are capable of building wealth? Why or why not?

What concerns do you have about retirement? What does retirement look like for you right now? Do you know who to talk to about your retirement? What goals do you have set for your retirement?

General Book Club Questions

Which chapter did you relate to the most? Why?

Share what you liked best and least about the book.

What other books does this book remind you of, and why?

What questions do you still have?

Share a favorite quote from the book. How did this quote impact you?

What feelings did this book bring about from your own story with money?

If you got the chance to ask the author one question, what would it be?

What are some new things you learned from this book?

What are some things you feel the author could've included in the book or taken away?

What did you already know about this topic before reading the book?

Who would you recommend should read this book?

What suggestions would you give to others before reading this book?

After reading this book, what is your next step?

Do you believe the book is relevant to readers today?

How did the book help you?

What are your thoughts about the cover and title of this book? What appealed to you, or what changes do you think should be made? How did the cover and title connect to the book?

The topic of the book is controversial as everyone has their own philosophy about finances. Do you believe the author presented the information well in an unbiased or biased way? If so, what biases were apparent?

Did you conduct additional research as you were reading the book?

Share one task you will complete or have completed as a result of reading this book.

Which writing activity helped you the most or was the most difficult?

Would you recommend this book to others? Why or why

not? What notions did you agree or disagree with in this

book? What surprising information did you find in this book?

What opinions have you changed or challenged since the reading of this book?

If you took the suggestions of this book, how would your life change?

Do you feel the information in this book is relevant to different cultures? How so or not?

What other books would you recommend that go along with this topic?

What are some main themes that are reflective in the book?

Would you read another book by this author?

Find YOUR Spark!

About the Publishing Support Services:

Motivational M.D. Publishing is a family-owned publishing company that assists aspiring authors publish books that heal, uplift, and inspire. It was founded by Dr. Jasmine Zapata who is an award-winning author, public health physician, empowerment speaker, mother, and wife. You can connect with Motivational M.D. Publishing team here: www.motivationalmdpublishing.com

John 3:16

Made in United States
Cleveland, OH
05 November 2026

47673665R00175